KS2 English Revision Gu

Alison Head

Welcome to the magical world of Wizard Whimstaff – a wise wizard with great English powers!

Whimstaff wants to pass on his powers to you. He has some friends to help him.

Miss Snufflebeam – a forgetful young dragon who is always getting confused...

Pointy – Whimstaff's smart goblin assistant...

And Mugly and Bugly – Pointy's lazy pet frogs, who prefer eating and snoozing to learning, but still have a few tricks to teach you.

Just work your way through the pages of this book and you too will become a real English wizard like Wizard Whimstaff and his friends!

Good luck, young wizard!

Letts

Contents

⭐ Spelling, punctuation and grammar

tick when completed

⭐ Writing

Writing (continued)

Reading

Apostrophes

Apostrophes are punctuation marks that can help us join words together and help show who things belong to. Super!

⭐ Contraction is just joining words!

Contraction of words is easy when you know how! We often join two words together by taking out one or more letters and putting an apostrophe in their place.

I am = I'm

she is = she's

we will = we'll

you are = you're

they have = they've

would not = wouldn't

cannot = can't

could have = could've

it is = it's

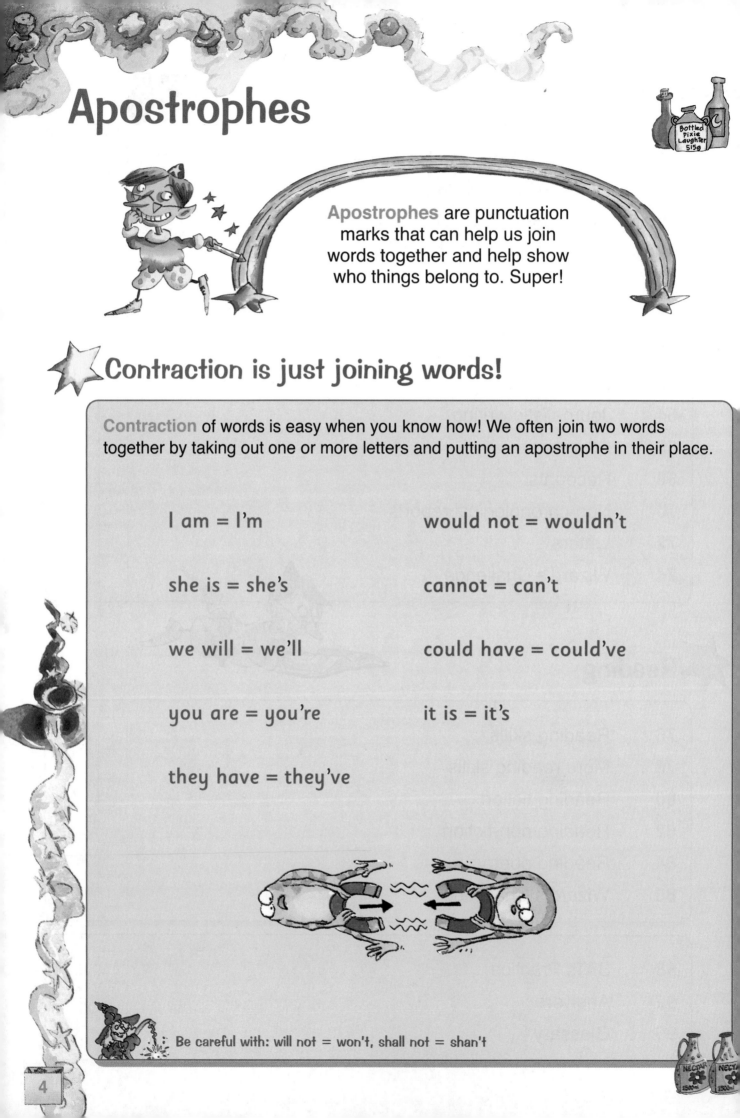

Be careful with: will not = won't, shall not = shan't

4

Apostrophes can also show who things belong to!

Apostrophes are super for showing who things belong to as well. There are just a few rules to follow.

Use an apostrophe, followed by **s**, for singular and plural nouns that don't end in **s**.

singular noun – a wizard's spells

plural noun – the children's sweets

Use **s**, then an apostrophe, for singular and plural nouns that end in **s**.

singular noun – Giles' shoes

plural noun – four flies' wings

If you want to say that something belongs to **it**, you never use an apostrophe. **It's** is only used to mean **it is**, e.g. a frog will hop off **its** lily pad if **it's** startled.

MAGIC WORDS
apostrophe · contraction
singular · plural · noun

Wizard's Practice

Workbook page 4

Add the missing apostrophe to each sentence.

1. Miss Snufflebeam can't breathe fire yet.
2. Mugly and Bugly doze because they're lazy.
3. Wizard Whimstaff's magic is amazing.
4. It's dark in the cave.
5. Six rat's tails went into the cauldron.

Unstressed vowels

Lots of words with two or more **syllables** contain **vowels** that are unstressed, or difficult to hear, when you say the word out loud. So how do I know how to spell them?

Silent vowels need extra practice!

In some words there are vowels that you can't hear at all. Other times, you can hear that there's a vowel there, but not which vowel it is. Can you help me practise them, so I remember how they're spelt?

frightening

memorable

mystery

factory

library

conference

In lots of these words, the unstressed vowel is **e**, followed by **r** or **n**.

Say them how they're spelt.

Words like these, that are not spelt how they sound, can be really tricky to spell. Try saying the word out loud, making sure that you say the unstressed vowel sound clearly. It might sound a bit silly, but it'll help you remember that tricky vowel. Dabracababra!

jewell – *e* – ry

hist – *o* – ry

diff – *e* – rence

lit – *e* – rature

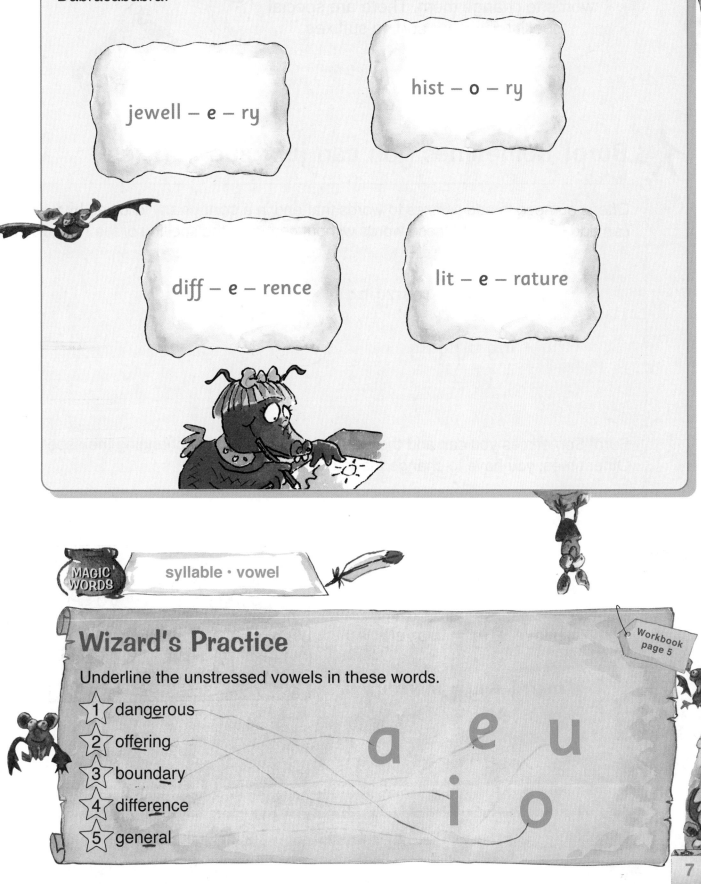

MAGIC WORDS | syllable · vowel

Wizard's Practice

Workbook page 5

Underline the unstressed vowels in these words.

1 danger<u>ou</u>s
2 off<u>e</u>ring
3 bound<u>a</u>ry
4 diff<u>e</u>rence
5 gen<u>e</u>ral

a e u
i o

7

Suffixes

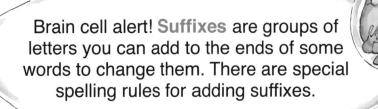

Brain cell alert! **Suffixes** are groups of letters you can add to the ends of some words to change them. There are special spelling rules for adding suffixes.

Burp! Sometimes you can just add suffixes!

Often you need to add suffixes to words that end in a **consonant** followed by **y**. You can add the suffix **ing** to these words without changing the spelling of the **root word**.

worry + ing = worrying

fly + ing = flying

Burp! Sometimes you can add the suffix **ly** to words without changing their spelling. Other times, you have to change the **y** to **i** first.

shy + ly = shyly

happy + ly = happily

brave + ly = bravely

merry + ly = merrily

Change y to i for suffixes ed, es and ness!

If you want to add **ed**, **es** or **ness** to a word that ends in a consonant then **y**, you have to change the **y** to **i** first. Slurp! Have a look at these.

cry + **ed** = cried

try + **es** = tries

friendly + **ness** = friendliness

MAGIC WORDS | suffix · consonant · root word

Wizard's Practice

Workbook page 6

Complete these word sums.

1. marry + ed = _married_
2. rely + ing = _relying_
3. steady + ly = _steadily_
4. silly + ness = _silliness_
5. dry + es = _dries_

Verb tenses

Past tense verbs are super for talking about things that have already happened!

⭐ Not all past tense verbs end in ed!

Lots of past tense verbs just end in **ed**, but some past tense verbs have different endings. You'll soon get the hang of it!

Regular ed ending:

walk ➡ walked

push ➡ pushed

Irregular past tense:

lose ➡ lost

find ➡ found

Some irregular verbs are spelt how they sound, like **lost**. They're easy to spell correctly. Some, like **found**, are a little harder. But don't worry, practice makes perfect!

Most irregular past tense verbs look similar to the present tense verb, but a few are completely different, e.g. go – went, is – was

Look for a super spelling pattern.

You'll soon get the hang of spelling irregular past tense verbs, if you can spot a spelling pattern.

Quite a few of these verbs end in **ght**.

catch → caught

think → thought

Another ending you'll see quite often is **ew**.

throw → threw

draw → drew

Some are nearly the same as the present tense verb, except for one letter.

win → won

sting → stung

A few verbs, like **read** and **cut**, are spelt just the same in the present tense and the past tense.

MAGIC WORDS past tense · verb · present tense

Wizard's Practice

Workbook page 7

Write down the past tense of these verbs.

1. hide _hid_
2. fight _fought_
3. bring _brought_
4. speak _spoke_
5. know _knew_

Speech

Did you know that there are two kinds of speech you might need to use in your writing? They're called **direct speech** and **reported speech**.

Direct speech is someone's actual words.

Let me tell you about direct speech, young wizard. That's where you write down the actual words that a character says. When you write direct speech, you need to use **speech marks** to show that it's someone's actual words. They go in pairs, at the beginning and at the end of the speech.

"I'm cleaning out the potions cupboard," said Pointy.

"Thank you," replied Wizard Whimstaff.

You need to say who's speaking too. You can do that before or after what they say. Look closely at where the speech marks and **comma** go in these sentences.

Wizard Whimstaff shouted, "Allakazan!"

Pointy replied, "Super!"

Begin on a fresh line each time a new character starts speaking. It makes it easier for your reader to work out who's speaking to whom.

12

Allakazan! No speech marks for reported speech!

Now, young wizard, let's look at reported speech. This is where you write what someone says, without using their actual words. It's not direct speech, so you don't need to use speech marks, but you still need to say who's speaking.

Pointy said he was cleaning out the potions cupboard.

The best stories usually contain a mixture of both direct and reported speech. Too much of either can be difficult or even boring to read, so try to use both.

Mugly and Bugly complained that they were hungry.

"How about a snack of juicy flies?" suggested Pointy.

Whether you're using direct or reported speech, try to avoid using the word **said** all the time. Try words like **asked, shouted, replied** or **giggled** instead.

MAGIC WORDS

direct speech · reported speech
speech marks · comma

Wizard's Practice

Workbook page 8

Put a tick by the sentences that contain direct speech.

1. Pointy said that the spell was super. ☐
2. Miss Snufflebeam said, "Oh dear! I've made a mistake." ✓
3. "This is hard work!" complained Mugly and Bugly. ✓
4. Wizard Whimstaff asked if Pointy had seen his hat. ☐
5. "Bugly, have you eaten all of the flies?" demanded Mugly. ✓
6. Miss Snufflebeam said that she wished she could breathe fire. ☐

Homophones

Can you help me understand **homophones**? They're words that sound the same, but are spelt differently and have a different meaning.

⭐ Watch out for homophones!

It's very easy to use the wrong homophone when you're writing, because homophones sound the same.

weight	wait
pain	pane
grate	great

Some of the words I use a lot have homophones and using the wrong one can completely change what I'm trying to write!

Night fell.

Knight fell.

⭐ Clever tricks can help you remember.

There are some homophones that I get wrong all the time, so Pointy has thought of a way to help me remember which one to use.

Which wand is Wizard Whimstaff's?

That one belongs to the witch.

I always get **which** and **witch** muddled up, but it helps if I remember that **which** is a question word, because it starts with **wh**, like **where**, **who**, and **why**. Dabracababa!

Mugly and Bugly take their nap over there.

This is another one I get wrong all the time. It helps to remember, though, that **there** looks very similar to **here**.

 Words that look or sound similar, but not exactly the same, can be difficult to remember too. Watch out for **where** and **were**, and **are** and **our**.

MAGIC WORDS | homophone

Workbook page 9

Wizard's Practice

Underline the correct homophone to complete each sentence.

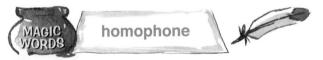

1. Mugly and Bugly ate / eight a whole jar of pickled snails.

2. Wizard Whimstaff reeds / reads his spells carefully before starting.

3. Pointy polished the crystal ball / bawl.

4. Miss Snufflebeam blew smoke four / for fun.

5. Wizard Whimstaff pawed / poured the potion into a bottle.

Nouns

Writing about things is easy when you know how! Nouns name things, people or groups, and there are different types of nouns for naming different types of things.

Nouns name things and feelings.

If you want to write about ordinary, everyday things, you use common nouns. Super!

The **frog** hopped.

I waved my **wand**.

Where is my magic **hat**?

Miss Snufflebeam is a **dragon**.

Abstract nouns name things that you cannot see or touch, like feelings or ideas.

Mugly and Mugly have a **fear** of soap.

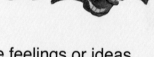

You have to show **courage** in the dark woods.

Wizard Whimstaff's **knowledge** is enormous!

 Nouns can be singular, which means just one; or plural, which means two or more. There are special spelling rules for plural nouns, which you can read about on page 28.

Nouns can name groups and people too!

Collective nouns describe groups of some nouns.

a shoal of fish   a pack of wolves

a pack of cards   a swarm of flies

a herd of cows

Proper nouns name important things, like specific people, places, the days of the week, and the months of the year. Unlike the other kinds of nouns, they always start with a capital letter, even if they appear in the middle of a sentence. Super!

Wizard Whimstaff stirred the cauldron.

Mugly and **Bugly** burped loudly.

Paris is the capital of **France**.

Friday is **April** fools' day.

Common nouns often have **a**, **an** or **the** before them.
You sometimes use them for abstract nouns too, but never for proper nouns.

MAGIC WORDS common noun · abstract noun
collective noun · proper noun

Workbook page 10

Wizard's Practice

Practice makes perfect! See if you can write down three examples of each of these:

1 singular noun _____ _____ _____

2 plural noun _____ _____ _____

3 abstract noun _____ _____ _____

4 collective noun _____ _____ _____

5 proper noun _____ _____ _____

Personal pronouns

> Allakazan! **Personal pronouns** are words you can sometimes use instead of nouns, to help make your writing flow better.

★ Personal pronouns stand in for nouns.

Listen carefully, young wizard. Personal pronouns can stand in for nouns when you're writing about people, to save you from having to keep using their names.

Look at how odd these sentences look.

> Miss Snufflebeam can only blow puffs of smoke. Miss Snufflebeam has not learnt to breathe fire yet, but Miss Snufflebeam is practising hard!

Hey presto! Now look at them again, using pronouns.

> Miss Snufflebeam can only blow puffs of smoke. **She** has not learnt to breathe fire yet, but **she** is practising hard!

We use different pronouns depending on the noun we're replacing. There are pronouns for females, males, groups, and things, for instance **I**, **me**, **he**, **she**, **him**, **her**, **we**, **they**, **it**, **us**, **them**.

> Mugly and Bugly hopped away and now I can't find **them**.

> The magic hat was dirty, so Pointy washed **it**.

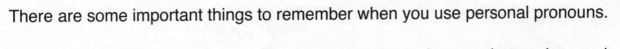

Don't forget the rules!

There are some important things to remember when you use personal pronouns.

If you want to replace a proper noun with a pronoun, make sure that you've used the proper noun at least once, so your reader knows who you're talking about!

Who does she think she is?

I have absolutely no idea, do you, young wizard? Without a proper noun, the sentence could be talking about any female!

You also have to be particularly careful if you're writing about two males, two females, or two things. If you call both of them **he**, **she** or **it**, your reader won't know which one you mean.

Wizard Whimstaff shouted to Pointy

and he ran to help him.

With this sentence, it's impossible to say for certain who did the running and helping.

 Personal pronouns don't usually have a capital letter, unless they're at the beginning of a sentence, but the exception is **I** which is always a capital letter.

MAGIC WORDS — personal pronoun

Wizard's Practice

Workbook page 11

Underline the personal pronouns in these sentences.

1. The cat appeared at the door, so <u>she</u> let it in.
2. Mugly and Bugly fell asleep after <u>they</u> had eaten.
3. Pointy can't remember where <u>he</u> put the cauldron.
4. Miss Snufflebeam was bored, so Pointy played a game with <u>her</u>.
5. Mugly and Bugly made a mess, so Pointy cleared up after <u>them</u>.

Paragraphs

Brain cell alert! We're always looking for ways to make life easier, and **paragraphs** are great news for readers and writers.

Paragraphs help you!

Slurp! Paragraphs break up long pieces of writing into smaller chunks, which is good, because we can never be bothered to write a whole page without taking a nap!

Paragraphs can save you time when you're writing, by helping you to organise your ideas.

In a short story, you might use one paragraph each for the beginning, the middle and the ending. In a **non-fiction** report, you could use a different paragraph for each topic.

Croak! Using paragraphs like this keeps all the sections in your writing roughly the same length.

It can help you to plan your time better in tests too. Just divide the time you have by the number of paragraphs you need to write. Then you'll know roughly how long to spend on each paragraph.

Some non-fiction writing can be written in bullet points instead.

Paragraphs help your readers too!

Burp! Paragraphs make life easier for your readers too.

A new paragraph tells your readers that you're going to start writing about something new or that a different character is doing something or speaking.

They're useful in a story if you want to start writing about something that's happening in a different setting too. In non-fiction writing, you should start a new paragraph if you want to change topic.

Whatever you're writing, if a paragraph is getting too long, think about breaking it in a sensible place and starting a new one. Leave a line between paragraphs, so your readers know that a new one is about to start.

Grub's up! Time for a snack! While we're eating, take a look at how the paragraphs were broken on this page you've just read.

 Some writers **indent** the first line of a new paragraph, which means starting a little way in from the edge of the page. First paragraphs shouldn't be indented.

MAGIC WORDS paragraph · non-fiction · indent

Wizard's Practice

Workbook page 12

Write **True** or **False** next to these statements about paragraphs.

1. You can use paragraphs to help you plan your writing. _True_
2. Each paragraph must cover the same topic as the one before. _False_
3. Writing without paragraphs can be very hard to read. _True_
4. You cannot have more than one sentence in a paragraph. _False_
5. Paragraphs help your reader to understand your writing. _True_

Connectives

Help! I know that connectives are words and phrases like **and**, **so** or **because**, but why do I need them?

⭐ Connectives make your writing flow.

Wizard Whimstaff always says that writing too many short, simple sentences can stop your writing from flowing nicely. That's because every time your reader gets to a full stop, they have to pause.

Mugly and Bugly looked into their food bowl. It was empty.

You can use connective words and phrases like **but**, **if** and **as a result** to join simple sentences together. They can help your writing flow better by allowing your reader to read for longer between pauses.

Mugly and Bugly looked into their food bowl, **but** it was empty.

 Simple sentences can be very effective if you use them sparingly. Try using them to draw attention to really important bits in your writing.

Add extra meaning.

Connectives don't just improve the structure of your writing. They can help you add extra meaning too. Different connectives have different meanings.

Cause and effect connectives show that one thing happens as a result of another.

> The cave was untidy, **so** Pointy tidied up.

They can also show that something happened in spite of something else.

> Miss Snufflebeam blew smoke in the cave,
> **although** she is not allowed to.

Time connectives show when something happened.

> Mugly and Bugly yawned **before** they fell asleep.

Dabracababa! Without time connectives, you would have to write everything down in exactly the order it happened, or it wouldn't make sense!

You can use a connective at the start of a sentence to link it to the one before. You can use them to link paragraphs, or even chapters, too!

> ... and with that, Mugly and Bugly went straight
> to sleep. **Meanwhile**, back at the cave...

Then is a time connective that is used far too much. Try using **after that, soon after,** or **suddenly** instead.

MAGIC WORDS
connective · simple sentence
full stop · phrase

Wizard's Practice

Workbook page 13

Underline the connectives in these sentences.

1. Mugly is fat, <u>but</u> Bugly is fatter.
2. Miss Snufflebeam was confused <u>because</u> the work was hard.
3. Wizard Whimstaff grabbed his wand <u>before</u> he cast the spell.
4. Pointy made Mugly and Bugly a snack <u>so</u> they would stop complaining.
5. The bats flew out of the cave <u>although</u> it was still light outside.

23

Adverbs

Hey presto! **Adverbs** work with verbs to say more about what someone or something is doing.

⭐ Adverbs add to verbs!

Let me tell you about adverbs. They help to paint a really vivid picture for your reader about what is happening. How? Because whilst verbs describe **what** is happening, adverbs describe **how** it happened.

Pointy ate.

Mugly and Bugly ate greedily.

Miss Snufflebeam ate daintily.

Allakazan! You can make adverbs work even harder for you by teaming them up with really powerful verbs.

Mugly and Bugly guzzled greedily.

Miss Snufflebeam nibbled daintily.

Hey presto! Can you see how the adverbs work with the verbs?

You can often turn **adjectives** into adverbs by adding the suffix **ly**, e.g. magical + ly = magically

Adverbs are great for describing dialogue too!

Now we're going to look at how you can use adverbs to describe your characters' **dialogue**. This means how your characters are speaking. What they say and how they say it tells us a lot about them and how they're feeling at that point in the story.

"Let's play a game," suggested Pointy, brightly.

"We're too tired!" complained
Mugly and Bugly, grumpily.

Without splendid verbs like **suggested** and **complained**, and magical adverbs, like **brightly** and **grumpily**, everything your characters say would sound the same. Very boring!

 Don't forget that what your characters say is just as important as how they say it! If you want them to seem happy or sad, the words they say need to reflect that.

MAGIC WORDS adverb · adjective · dialogue

Wizard's Practice

Workbook page 14

Pick an adverb from the cauldron to complete these sentences.

curiously

excitedly   sulkily

proudly   politely

1 "Let's have a party!" exclaimed Miss Snufflebeam, _excitedly_.

2 "Have you seen Mugly and Bugly?" asked Pointy, _curiously_.

3 "Please may I have a drink?" asked Miss Snufflebeam, _politely_.

4 "We're hungry!" grumbled Mugly and Bugly, _sulkily_.

5 "Look at my wonderful new cloak," said Wizard Whimstaff, _proudly_.

Prepositions

You'll soon get the hang of using **prepositions**! They're words that describe how one thing relates to another.

⭐ Know where you are with prepositions.

Describing where things are is easy when you know how! Lots of prepositions describe **where** things are in relation to each other. We can use them with nouns or pronouns.

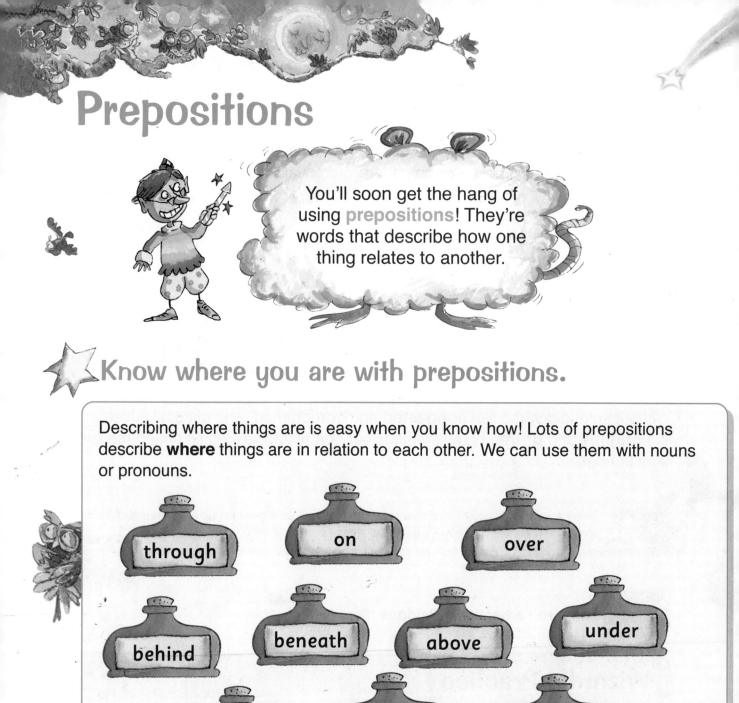

through

on

over

behind

beneath

above

under

towards

across

along

The potion is **in** the bottle.

The witch sat **on** her broomstick.

Mugly hopped **over** Bugly.

Prepositions often go before the noun they relate to.

 There are about 150 prepositions in the English language and we use them all the time. The prepositions **of**, **to** and **in** are among the ten most frequently used words.

Prepositions do other things too!

People tend to think that prepositions just tell us where things are, but they can also give us information about **when** something happened. Super!

before

pending

after

during

until

Mugly and Bugly fell asleep **after** their snack.

Pointy tidied up **before** he went out.

Miss Snufflebeam dreamt she was a princess **during** the night.

That's not all either. Prepositions help us to understand countless other ways things relate to each other too. You'll soon get the hang of it!

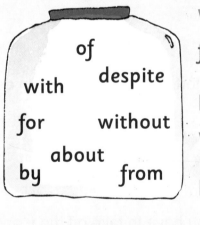

of

with

despite

for

without

about

by

from

Wizard Whimstaff received a letter **from** an old friend.

Miss Snufflebeam's story book was written **by** a fairy.

Pointy made a snack **for** Mugly and Bugly.

MAGIC WORDS   preposition

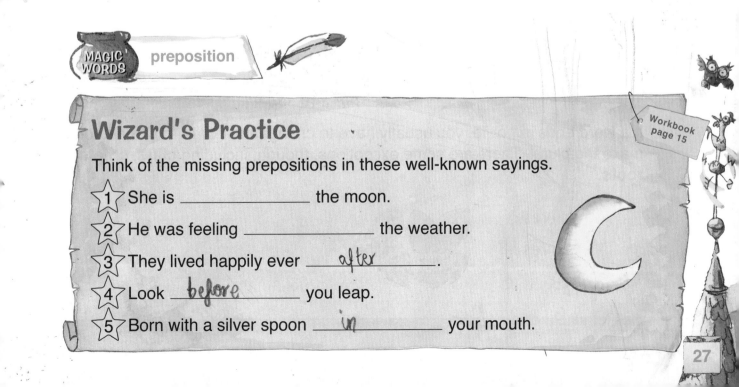

Wizard's Practice

Workbook page 15

Think of the missing prepositions in these well-known sayings.

1. She is _____ the moon.

2. He was feeling _____ the weather.

3. They lived happily ever __*after*__.

4. Look __*before*__ you leap.

5. Born with a silver spoon __*in*__ your mouth.

Plurals

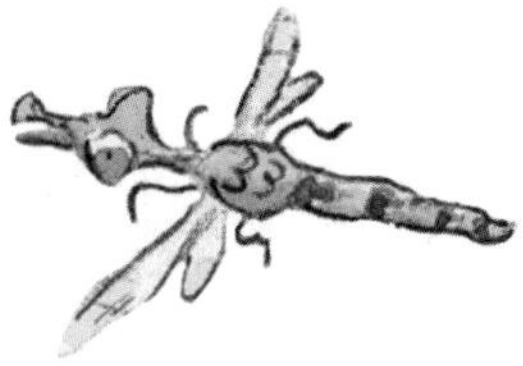

Slurp! Like us, all the best things come in twos! Plural means two or more of something. Plural nouns usually have a different spelling.

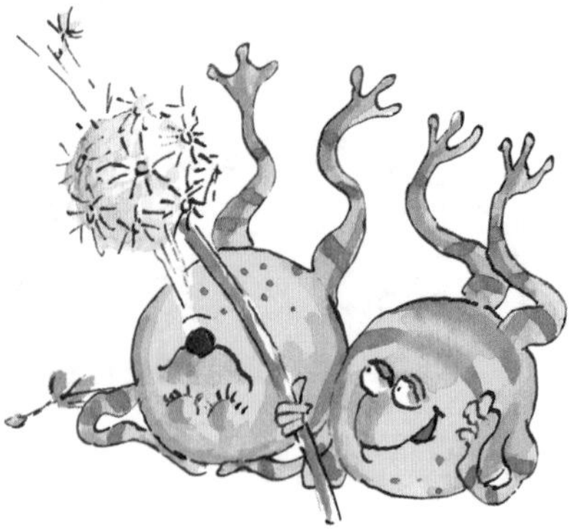

Most plural nouns are easy to spell!

Croak! Most of the time, you spell plural nouns by adding **s** to the singular noun.

frog**s**

snack**s**

Words ending in **s**, **x**, **z**, **sh** or **ch** take a bit more effort. Most of them end in **es**.

witch**es**

fox**es**

With words ending in a consonant followed by **y**, you have to take off the **y** and add **ies** to make the plural.

jell**ies**

fl**ies**

If a word ends in **f** or **fe**, you usually have to change the **f** or **fe** to **v**, then add **es** to make the plural. There are some exceptions, though, including **cliffs**, **chiefs** and **roofs**.

cal**ves**

lea**ves**

Some words don't follow the rules!

Brain cell alert! Bet you thought we'd finished! Unfortunately, not all words follow the rules.

Some words change completely in the plural.

mouse	mice
person	people
cactus	cacti
child	children

Some words are the same, whether they're singular or plural.

sheep	sheep
aircraft	aircraft
series	series
deer	deer

Lots of the words that are the same in the singular and the plural are the names of fish! Tuna, salmon, trout and bream are good examples.

Wizard's Practice

Workbook page 16

Write down the plurals of these words.

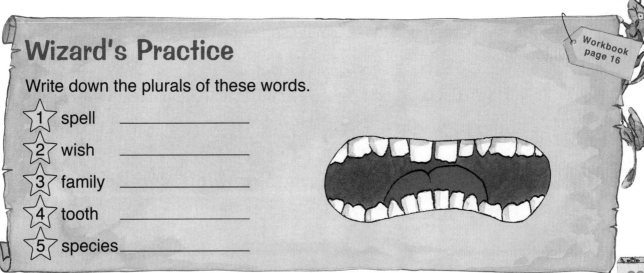

1 spell _____

2 wish _____

3 family _____

4 tooth _____

5 species _____

Sentences

Can you help me remember the difference between **compound sentences** and **complex sentences**? It's all to do with how the **clauses** work, I think.

⭐ Building compound sentences.

Abracadada! You can join two simple sentences together with a special type of connective called a **conjunction**. Using conjunctions to join simple sentences together can make your writing flow better, because they allow your reader to read for longer without having to pause at a full stop.

Each of the simple sentences becomes a clause in a new sentence. A clause is a distinct part of a sentence and usually contains a verb.

> Wizard Whimstaff waved his wand. The mouse disappeared.

> Wizard Whimstaff waved his wand **and** the mouse disappeared.

In the sentence above, each clause makes sense on its own and they each have the same weight in the sentence. This type of sentence is called a compound sentence.

Can you see how putting these simple sentences together makes a compound sentence?

> Pointy cleaned the cave. Mugly and Bugly made it messy again.

> Pointy cleaned the cave, **but** Mugly and Bugly made it messy again.

Complex sentences have a subordinate clause.

In complex sentences, one of the clauses is called a subordinate clause, because it adds information to the main clause, but wouldn't make sense on its own.

Yawning sleepily, Miss Snufflebeam went to bed.

subordinate clause   main clause

Do you see how the subordinate clause adds information?

Abracadada! You can often put a subordinate clause in the middle of a sentence too, with commas around it. This is called an embedded clause.

Mugly burped loudly. He is Bugly's twin.

Mugly, who is Bugly's twin, burped loudly.

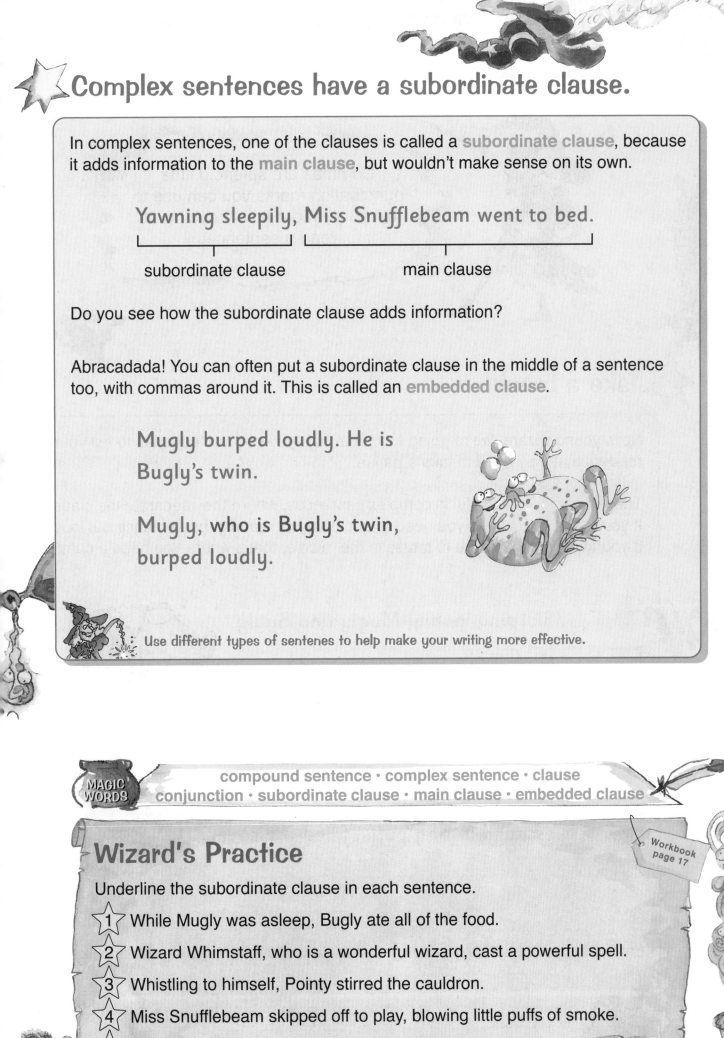

Use different types of sentenes to help make your writing more effective.

Workbook page 17

MAGIC WORDS

compound sentence · complex sentence · clause
conjunction · subordinate clause · main clause · embedded clause

Wizard's Practice

Underline the subordinate clause in each sentence.

1. While Mugly was asleep, Bugly ate all of the food.
2. Wizard Whimstaff, who is a wonderful wizard, cast a powerful spell.
3. Whistling to himself, Pointy stirred the cauldron.
4. Miss Snufflebeam skipped off to play, blowing little puffs of smoke.
5. Mugly and Bugly, croaking loudly, hopped onto a lily pad.

Commas

Commas are splendid little punctuation marks you can use to tell your reader how they should read a sentence.

Take a break!

Now, young wizard, we're going to look at how you can use commas to tell your readers that they need to take a pause.

They're particularly useful in complex sentences, where they separate the clauses. If you're not sure where you need to put them, try reading the sentence out loud. If you find it makes sense to pause in the middle, that's where you need a comma.

Slurping loudly, Mugly and Bugly fell asleep.

Miss Snufflebeam's smoke, which escaped in tiny puffs, filled the cave.

Let me tell you about other ways commas can be useful to young wizards like you.

Remember that as well as commas, you can use connectives like **so**, **and** or **in the end** to join clauses.

Commas have other uses too!

First, let's look at how commas can help you separate things in a list. You just pop one in between each item on the list, to separate them. The only time you don't use a comma is before the final **and** in the list.

> For my new spell I need a spider's web, a rat's sneeze, three whiskers from a black cat and a purple mushroom.

Next, let's look at dialogue. When a character speaks, you need to use speech marks at the beginning and end of what they say. You also need to use a comma to separate what they say from the rest of the sentence.

Sometimes the speech comes first.

> "Time for a snack," said Mugly and Bugly.

Sometimes the speech comes at the end of the sentence.

> Pointy replied, "I'll see if we have any swamp bugs left."

Either way, the comma comes before the speech punctuation.

Remember, if the speech comes first, and it ends with a **question mark** or **exclamation mark**, you don't use a comma as well.

MAGIC WORDS question mark · exclamation mark

Wizard's Practice

Workbook page 18

Add the missing commas to these sentences.

1. Blowing puffs of smoke Miss Snufflebeam skipped out of the cave.
2. "Mugly and Bugly have made a mess again " grumbled Pointy.
3. Wizard Whimstaff with his wand held high said the magic words.
4. Mugly and Bugly ate six flies three snails and a plate of swamp slime.
5. Pointy washed up the potion bottles singing cheerfully.

Capital letters

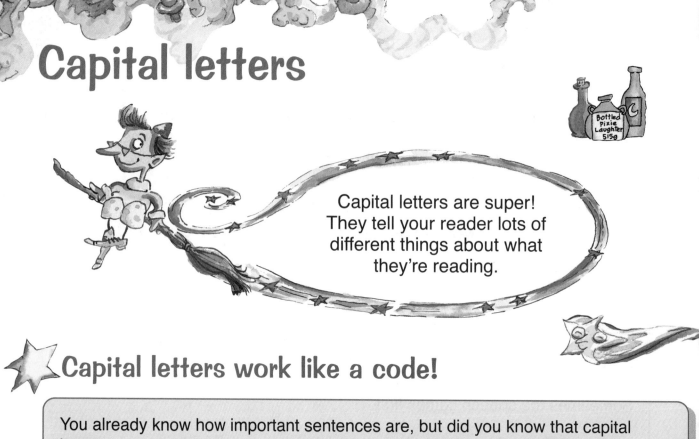

Capital letters are super! They tell your reader lots of different things about what they're reading.

⭐ Capital letters work like a code!

You already know how important sentences are, but did you know that capital letters are one of the main ways your reader knows that a new sentence has begun?

You have to use a capital letter at the start of a sentence, so whenever you have used a full stop, exclamation mark, or question mark, you have to start again afterwards with a capital letter.

The wizard peered into the cauldron. What was making that awful smell? Bang! The potion exploded in a cloud of silver stars, leaving the wizard transformed into a mouse!

Before you put a capital letter in the middle of a sentence, think carefully! Some words do need to start with a capital letter, but if you use one where you don't need to, your readers will think that you're starting a new sentence.

 You might not always use capital letters and full stops when you're texting someone, or writing an email to a friend, but you should always use them in your school work.

⭐ Proper nouns need capital letters too!

The names of people, places and things like the days of the week and months of the year are called proper nouns. They're the names of special things, so they need to start with a capital letter too. Super!

Mugly

Wednesday

London

April

Sometimes you might use a pronoun like **she**, **it** and **me**, in the place of a proper noun. Usually pronouns don't start with a capital letter, unless they're at the start of a sentence. The only very important exception to this is **I** which is always a capital letter, wherever it appears in a sentence.

It was dark, so I lit a candle.

Wizard's Practice

Workbook page 19

Practice makes perfect! Circle the correct word from the pair of words in each sentence.

1. Miss snufflebeam / Snufflebeam blew a little puff of smoke.

2. It / it was dark at the back of the cave.

3. Last Tuesday / tuesday Wizard Whimstaff bought a new magic wand.

4. Pointy's aunt lives in transylvania / Transylvania.

5. Mugly said Bugly ate all the flies, but I / i don't believe him.

Antonyms

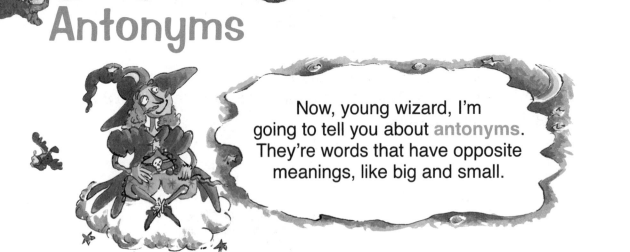

Now, young wizard, I'm going to tell you about **antonyms**. They're words that have opposite meanings, like big and small.

Antonyms are just opposites!

Allakazan! Antonyms are useful for describing the differences between things. There are different types of antonyms, which work in slightly different ways, to help you get just the right effect in your writing.

Some antonyms are absolute opposites.

kind	↔	unkind
happy	↔	unhappy
behave	↔	misbehave

Some describe the relationship between two things.

wizard	↔	apprentice
parent	↔	child
buy	↔	sell

Others are at either end of a range of words, with variations in between.

cold	←	**warm**	→	hot
wet	←	**damp**	→	dry
large	←	**medium**	→	small

All of them are really useful for describing contrasts between things in your writing.

 Lots of great stories are based on opposites, like **Beauty and the Beast.**

Prefixes can make antonyms!

Now I'm going to show you how lots of the antonyms we use all the time are made by taking a word and adding a prefix to it. **Prefixes** are groups of letters you can add to the beginning of some words to change their meaning.

Hey presto! The prefixes **im**, **un**, **dis**, **mis**, **anti** and **in** can all be added to some words to create antonyms.

possible	➜	**im**possible
done	➜	**un**done
appear	➜	**dis**appear
conduct	➜	**mis**conduct
social	➜	**anti**social
direct	➜	**in**direct

Allakazan! Like all prefixes, you can add **im**, **un**, **dis**, **mis**, **anti** and **in** to the beginning of a word without changing the spelling first.

Look out for the suffixes **less** and **ful**, which are often found at the end of antonyms like **useless** and **useful**; and **careless** and **careful**.

MAGIC WORDS   antonym · prefix

Wizard's Practice

Workbook page 20

Hey presto! Now see if you can match up these words with a prefix from my hat to make antonyms.

1 _____ + polite = _____

2 _____ + approve = _____

3 _____ + decisive = _____

4 _____ + certain = _____

5 _____ + septic = _____

un

anti

in

dis   im

Wizard's Challenge

 Apostrophes

Slurp! Add the apostrophes to this sentence.

> Miss Snufflebeams smoke got into Pointys eyes, so he didnt see the crystal ball until hed knocked it off its stand.

 Unstressed vowels

Croak! Now see if you can underline the unstressed vowels in these words.

a parliament   **c** reference

b different   **d** natural

 Verb tenses

Brain cell alert! Circle the correct past tense version of these present tense verbs.

a run   runned / ran

b joke   joked / jokeed

c creep   creeped / crept

4 Connectives

Brain cell alert! Can you think of a suitable connective to complete this sentence?

Miss Snufflebeam won't be able to blow smoke
_____ she's older.

5 Adverbs

Burp! Now draw lines to match up these verbs with suitable adverbs.

a whispered   pleadingly

b shouted   shyly

c asked   angrily

6 Plurals

Sort these words into the correct lily pad, depending on how you make the plural.

a lady

b box

c train

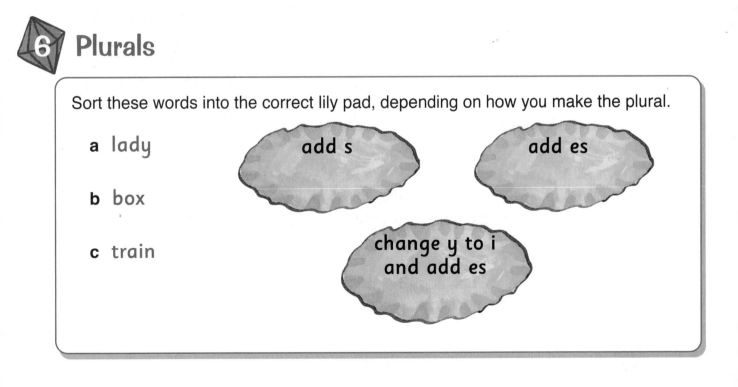

add s

add es

change y to i
and add es

I often get in a muddle when I'm writing **fiction**, so I find it helps to write a plan first.

⭐ Plans keep you focused.

Thinking about a whole story at once is confusing! Plans break stories up into sections, so you can think about what needs to go into each section, and make sure that all the sections fit together properly.

	opening
+	build-up
+	dilemma
+	events
+	resolution
=	fantastic story!

Help! Writing stories in a test can be scary, but writing a plan can actually save you time by keeping you focused. You'll get extra marks too, because your story will be better.

In a 45-minute test, aim to spend about 10 minutes on your plan. In a 20-minute test, try not to spend more than 5 minutes planning.

Use your plan to jot down any special words you might use to describe your characters and settings.

Stories need a structure!

Story structure is important, so I've planned my story in five sections.

Opening: Introduce your characters and setting.

> Wendy is a young witch who borrows her mother's broomstick, without asking.

Build-up: Explain the events that lead up to the big dilemma in the story. You can give your readers more information about your characters here too.

> Wendy flies to the top of the mountain on the broomstick, parks it, and goes exploring.

Dilemma: This is really the heart of your story, and explains the problem your characters have to solve.

> The broomstick flies off without her. How will she get it back?

Events: What happens next? How do your characters try to solve the problems?

> Wendy tries to climb down, but the mountain is too steep. Then she finds a dragon's nest.

Resolution: Have your characters been able to solve the problem?

> The dragon carries Wendy safely down the mountain and she promises not to borrow things again without asking.

Cliffhanger endings, where the reader never finds out what happens, can be very effective.

MAGIC WORDS | fiction

Wizard's Practice

Workbook page 21

Think of something else, for the 'events' part of the plan, that could happen to Wendy to get her home safely. _____

_____

_____

41

Special effects

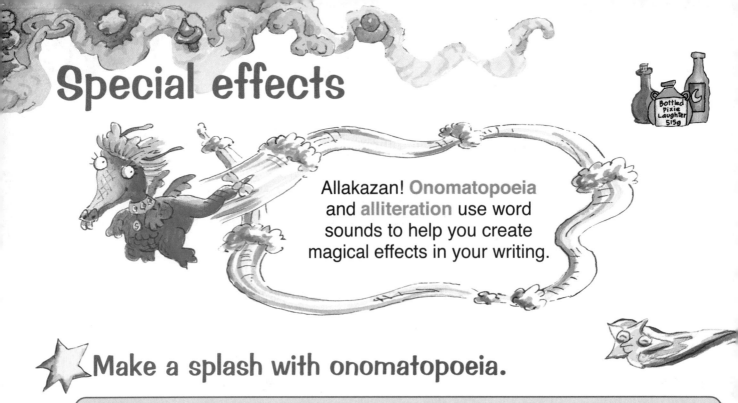

Allakazan! **Onomatopoeia** and **alliteration** use word sounds to help you create magical effects in your writing.

⭐ Make a splash with onomatopoeia.

Hey presto! Onomatopoeias can really help to bring your writing to life. They're words which sound just like the noise they describe.

slurp

burp

croak

Onomatopoeias make it much easier for your reader to imagine what is happening in your story. They can also save you time and make your writing flow better, because you only need one word to describe a sound, rather than lots.

The balloon burst, making a really loud noise.

The balloon popped.

Onomatopoeia works particularly well in fiction and poetry, or anywhere you want to add a bit of humour.

Alliteration works wonders too!

Let me tell you about another splendid trick that has to do with the sounds of words.

Alliteration is where the first sound in a series of words is the same, or very similar.

> **Pointy paints pleasing pictures.**

With alliteration, it's the first sound of the words that matters, not the first letter, because some letters can make more than one sound.

> **Philip fanned his face.** ✔

> **Philip pulled the pony.** ✘

Alliteration works really well in fiction writing, for drawing attention to important details. It's also often used in poetry and in newspaper headlines.

Tongue-twisters like the famous **Peter Piper picked...** use lots of alliteration, because it's hard to keep saying the same sound over and over again.

MAGIC WORDS onomatopoeia · alliteration

Wizard's Practice

Workbook page 22

Read these sentences and work out whether they contain onomatopoeia or alliteration. Write **O** or **A** in the box.

1. The fat frogs flopped into the water. ☐
2. Pointy clattered down the stairs. ☐
3. Miss Snufflebeam chattered happily. ☐
4. Wizard Whimstaff worked willingly. ☐
5. Pointy poured the potion proudly. ☐

More special effects

Personification and simile are techniques that use comparisons between things to help you create brilliant effects in your writing. Super!

Personification brings things to life!

Personification is a writing technique where human characteristics are used to describe things that are not alive. It can help to bring your settings to life for your readers, by making it easier to imagine what they are like. You'll soon get the hang of it!

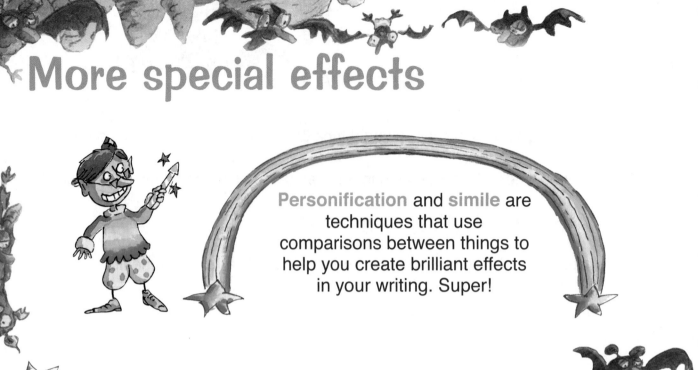

The boy crept silently into the **waiting darkness**.
The **moon gazed** down on him as he walked
through the **whispering trees**.

Describing the darkness, the moon and the trees as if they were alive and knew that the boy was there, adds suspense and help us to imagine how he might be feeling.

Personification is great for creating a mood in your writing. The **whispering trees** create tension, or you could have a **smiling sun** instead, which would create a much lighter mood.

Similes can make your writing sparkle like a jewel!

Simile is another clever technique that uses comparison to help create a picture for your readers. Similes compare one thing to another, using the words **as** or **like**.

sleeping **like** a baby

as busy **as** a bee

There are lots of familiar similes that people use all the time. If you use them in your writing, people will know exactly what you mean and will be able to imagine easily what your characters are doing.

You can also make up your own similes, which will add humour to your writing. Super!

Think carefully about the characteristics of the thing you want to describe, then try to think of something else that has similar characteristics.

skin like an old handbag

People often get simile confused with **metaphor**. With metaphor, you say that something **is** something else, e.g. **she is a star**.

MAGIC WORDS   personification · simile · metaphor

Wizard's Practice

Workbook page 23

Practice makes perfect! Complete these well-known similes.

1. as pretty as a _____
2. as gentle as a _____
3. run like the _____
4. as quiet as a _____
5. swim like a _____

Choosing language

Just because we're lazy doesn't mean that you can be! Choosing brilliant words is very important. Adjectives work hard to make your writing interesting and synonyms save you from having to use the same tired words again and again.

Adjectives are just describing words.

Croak! Adjectives are words that describe nouns. There are different types of adjectives to do different jobs.

Comparative adjectives help you to compare things.

Mugly is fat but Bugly is fatter.

Lots of comparative adjectives end in **er**, but some are written in different ways. You need to be careful to use the correct word; you wouldn't say **more better** or **comfortabler**, so why write it?

famous	more famous
good	better
expensive	less expensive

Burp! There's more to come! **Superlative adjectives** describe the fullest possible extent of a particular quality.

fast	fastest
great	greatest
big	biggest

Most superlative adjectives end in **est**, but there are some exceptions. Also, comparative adjectives that use **more** or **less** will use **most** or **least** when they're superlative adjectives.

Try to think of synonyms for boring adjectives, like nice or bad.

Synonyms are just words with similar meanings.

Brain cell alert! When you're writing, don't just use the first word that pops into your head. Think about whether there's a better word, with a similar meaning, that you could use.

Words with similar meanings are called synonyms. Lots of adjectives have synonyms, and choosing the right one can help you describe exactly what something or someone is like. Burp! Grub's up! Look at the different ways we could describe our snack.

yummy	tasty
delicious	scrumptious
appetising	mouthwatering

Is it time for a snooze yet? Verbs have synonyms too. Some verbs are more powerful than others, because they help your readers to imagine exactly what your characters are doing. So instead of just using the verb sleep to describe our nap, you could think of a more interesting verb.

sleep	slumber
snooze	rest
doze	hibernate

A **thesaurus** is a special book that lists synonyms of different words.

MAGIC WORDS

synonym · comparative adjective
superlative adjective · thesaurus

Wizard's Practice

Workbook page 24

Slurp! Think of synonyms for these words.

1. old _____
2. laugh _____
3. walk _____
4. courageous _____
5. break _____

Formal and informal language

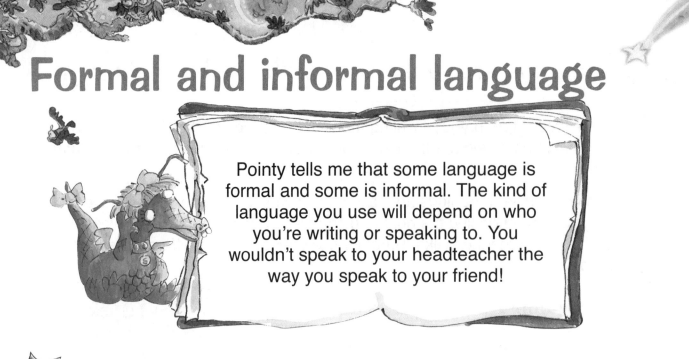

Pointy tells me that some language is formal and some is informal. The kind of language you use will depend on who you're writing or speaking to. You wouldn't speak to your headteacher the way you speak to your friend!

Informal language is what we use with our friends.

Informal language is the kind of language we use with our family and friends.

We usually use just their first names, or we might say Mum or Dad.

We might also use contractions, like **I'm**, **we'll** or **you're**, instead of **I am**, **we will** or **you are**.

Informal language tends to use active verbs, rather than passive verbs. Active verbs identify the person doing the action.

Ben gave me the book for my birthday.

I will collect you this afternoon.

Grace is coming round for tea.

Slang words or phrases that we use with friends is informal language too. The kind of language we use when we text or email each other is so informal that we often don't bother about punctuation or spelling, to save time.

 All language changes over time, but informal language often changes more quickly than formal language. The arrival of email and texting has brought about a whole new way of writing informally.

Formal language is for people we know less well.

Help! I always get in a muddle with formal language. I think it's the kind of language we use for talking or writing to people we don't know as well as our family and friends, or who are older than us, like Wizard Whimstaff.

We tend to use a more formal way of addressing people like this.

Sir   Ms Jackson   Dr Khan

Formal writing doesn't usually use contractions, so you would write **do not** and **cannot**, instead of **don't** and **can't**.

Formal language often uses passive verbs, which describe the action, rather than who's doing it.

Your account **will be credited**.

Your membership **has been renewed**.

You **have been entered** into a prize draw.

Formal language doesn't have any slang, and if you write a formal letter or email, you need to use the same capital letters and punctuation you would use in your school work.

 You can read more about writing formal and informal letters later in the book.

MAGIC WORDS   active verb · passive verb

Wizard's Practice

Workbook page 25

Write **Formal** or **Informal** after each of these sentences.

1. Fancy a swim?   _____

2. Your confirmation slip will be forwarded to you.   _____

3. r u ok?   _____

4. See you later!   _____

5. Overnight parking is prohibited.   _____

Openings and endings

Every section of a story matters, but if you write a weak opening your reader may never get as far as the magical ending you have planned!

⭐ Openings are your chance to make a first impression!

Your opening sets the scene and introduces your characters. You need to make it really gripping, so your readers will want to keep on reading. It's easy when you know how!

There are different ways you can start your story.

You could start it with a description of your setting, with lots of strong adjectives and adverbs, and techniques like personification and alliteration to bring it to life.

The village crouched in the valley.   **personification**
Carefully kept cottages crowded
round the little pond.   **alliteration**

Or you could start with a description of your character. Remember those adjectives!

Katie ran along the muddy track from the
farmhouse where she lived with her family,
pushing her curly hair out of her big blue eyes as
she went.

Read as many short stories as you can, to see how other people use story openings.

The ending is just as important as the opening!

There are lots of different ways your stories can end, but a good ending will make your reader carry on thinking after they've finished reading.

In a happy ending, all of the problems in the story are resolved, and the characters are safe and happy. This is the classic ending used in fairy tales, and think how long people have been reading those!

> **The prince and princess were married and lived happily ever after.**

You might want your story to tell a moral lesson at the end, like a **fable**. Sometimes writers punish nasty characters at the end of the story.

> **As Sam watched from the headmaster's office, the coach left for the school trip without him.**

In a cliffhanger ending, the characters are simply left in a difficult situation, and the reader is left wondering what might happen next. Super!

> **As Ben climbed onto the train that would take him away forever, the sun set slowly over the mountains.**

MAGIC WORDS — fable

Wizard's Practice

Workbook page 26

Write new endings for these well-known fairy stories, under the existing ones.

Fairy tale	Existing ending
Little Red Riding Hood	The woodcutter rescues Red and Grandma from the wolf.
	_____
	_____
Cinderella	The glass slipper fits Cinderella, so she marries the prince.
	_____
	_____

Characters

Characters are the people in your story and getting them right is really tricky. If you do a good job, though, your readers will be interested in what happens to them and will want to keep reading!

⭐ Work your characters into your plan.

There's such a lot to think about when you're writing about characters. You need to think about your characters right at the start, when you're writing your plan.

How old would they be if they were real? How would they talk? What might they say to the other characters in the story? All of these things will affect what they say and do in the story.

Mugly and Bugly

- say 'burp!', 'croak' and 'slurp' a lot
- green frogs
- sleep most of the time
- twins – always together
- demand regular snacks
- fat and lazy
- rude to everyone

Nasty characters can work just as well as kind, friendly ones. If you decide what they'll be like at the start, it'll be easier to plan what will happen to them in the story.

Don't be tempted to have too many characters in your story, or you won't have space to describe them all properly. Two or three works best in most short stories.

Descriptions bring your characters to life!

Try to use powerful adjectives to describe your characters, along with powerful verbs and adverbs to talk about what they do. You can also try techniques like simile and metaphor to help your reader to build up a picture of what they're like.

Too much description of what your characters look like can get boring, though. Only mention things that help the reader to understand what they're like.

> The strange man wrapped a huge, dark cloak around his hunched shoulders, and peered out with piercing eyes.

Oops! I nearly forgot! What your characters say, and how they say it, is really important too. So if your character is angry, for example, try using short sentences and exclamation marks to make it seem like he's shouting.

> "Get out!"

If you decide to base a character on someone you know, make sure you change their name and a few of the details, so they don't recognise themselves!

Wizard's Practice

Workbook page 27

Imagine that you're writing a story about a famous footballer scoring the winning goal for his team. Write down five words or phrases you could use in the story to describe him.

_____

_____

_____

_____

Settings

Now we're going to look at how getting your setting right will help to make your story more convincing and full of atmosphere.

⭐ Allakazan! Create your perfect setting!

When you're describing a setting, you have some important decisions to make!

What does it smell like?

What time of day is it?

What does it look like?

What is the weather like?

What does it sound like?

Hey presto! Look at your story plan and think carefully about what would work best. A spooky story set in a crowded park on a sunny afternoon wouldn't be very believable!

Often you'll only need one setting for a short story, but if you decide to have two, you'll need to think about how you'll move from one setting to the other, so your reader understands what's going on.

Connectives like **meanwhile, back at home** or **at that moment,** will help to ensure that your readers keep up with the action. Try starting a new paragraph when you change location, too.

You don't necessarily have to have whole sentences of setting description. Try adding a detail here and there when you're writing about the action.

Tom searched for a way out, rattling the ancient windows in their rotting frames.

Description brings your setting to life!

Once you've chosen your setting, you need to think of a really effective way to describe it.

Think of some strong adjectives to describe the sights, sounds and smells, and use adverbs to help describe what's happening. You should also think about using a technique like personification or onomatopoeia, for extra impact.

> The wind whistled down the deserted street. The branches of the trees waved at Jemma as she hurried by, and crisp autumn leaves scuttled along behind her.

If you have two contrasting settings, think about antonyms you could use to emphasise the differences, e.g. contrast a bright corridor with a gloomy passage.

Wizard's Practice

Workbook page 28

Draw lines to match up each setting with a suitable description.

1. a hospital ward   crunching pebbles

2. a woodland   pointy pencils poised

3. a beach   lush leaves

4. a classroom   excited splashing

5. a swimming pool   gleaming tiles

Narrators

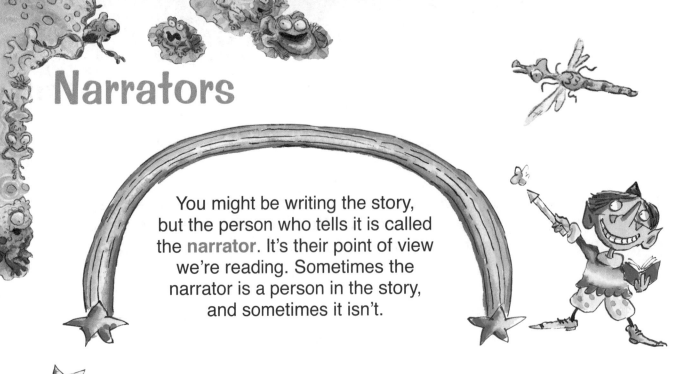

You might be writing the story, but the person who tells it is called the **narrator**. It's their point of view we're reading. Sometimes the narrator is a person in the story, and sometimes it isn't.

The narrator can be a character in the story.

Deciding who your narrator should be is easy when you know how! Usually, if the narrator is a character in a story, he or she will be the main character. Everything in the story will be written from their point of view, so your readers will get to know them really well. Super!

On the other hand, because everything is based on their thoughts and opinions, it can be harder for readers to get to know and understand the other characters.

If your narrator is in the story, you can use the past tense or the present tense, or a mixture of both!

I don't understand why she hates me. I invited her to my party but she didn't come.

Sometimes stories like this are written as if they were diary entries written by the character.

 In non-fiction, people often write about their lives and experiences, taking on the role of narrator. This is called autobiography.

Sometimes the narrator isn't in the story at all!

Often, the narrator isn't part of the story at all. They simply tell us what happens, without making any comment on who's right or wrong.

This type of narrator can work better because they can 'see' all of the characters all of the time. They also know things that the characters might not know yet.

So while Snow White might not know that the wicked queen wants to kill her, we do. It adds suspense to the story as we wait to find out what will happen.

When the narrator isn't in the story, you have to use the past tense.

> They crossed the old railway line
> and headed for the trees.
>
> **not**
>
> They are crossing the old railway
> line and heading for the trees.

 MAGIC WORDS 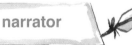 narrator

Wizard's Practice

Workbook page 29

Write out the narrator's sentences again as if she were not a character in the story.

1. I hate my little brother. _____

2. He drives me mad! _____

3. He's always stealing my things. _____

4. He makes our whole house a mess. _____

5. I do think he's cute when he's asleep, though! _____

_____

Genre

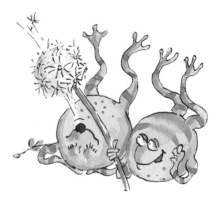

Brain cell alert! **Genre** means a type of writing. There are fiction genres, like science fiction and westerns; and non-fiction genres, like instructions and adverts.

Genre just means story type!

Listen up! Different types of stories tend to have different structures and different types of characters.

Fantasy quests

Characters
often mythical characters, like dragons, trolls and unicorns

What happens?
a long and perilous journey, often in search of something

Structure
one challenge after another, to be overcome by the hero

Action adventures

Characters
a good action hero and a villain

What happens?
the hero pursues the villain; lots of dangerous, high-speed activity

Structure
there's often a quarrel between the hero and villain early on, and this goes on throughout the action

Thrillers

Characters
often ordinary people who find themselves in the middle of a mystery

What happens?
the characters find themselves in a scary or dangerous place, and unexpected events happen

Structure
atmosphere is very important; often the dilemma is rather mysterious and you have to wait right until the end to find out a secret.

Thinking about genre can help you to write a good story, but make sure your plot is original.

There are genres in non-fiction writing too!

Croak! Genre is just a name for different types of writing, so there are non-fiction genres too.

Different non-fiction genres use language differently.

Burp! Have a read of this, while we grab a snack!

Genre	Purpose	Language
journalistic writing	to inform	newspaper reports should not take sides; may use creative techniques like alliteration, simile or onomatopoeia
instructions	to tell the reader how to do something	clarity is very important; may use technical terms
adverts	to inform and persuade	will include information about location, prices; may use lots of superlative adjectives and creative techniques

With non-fiction writing, the purpose of the writing is very important, and it will affect how much you need to write, the structure of your work, and the kind of language you use.

There's lots more information about different types of non-fiction writing later in the book.

 **MAGIC WORDS**   genre

Wizard's Practice

Workbook page 30

Draw lines to match up these sentences with the genre you think they belong to.

1. The unicorn disappeared into the forest.   Fiction: thriller

2. Use a ratchet to undo bolt F.   Non-fiction: advert

3. Available now at a special introductory price.   Non-fiction: instructions

4. Angry residents met council officials on Wednesday.   Fiction: fantasy quest

5. The warehouse door slammed behind them.   Non-fiction: journalistic writing

Balanced arguments

Let me tell you about **balanced arguments**, young wizard. They just set out the views on either side of a debate, so people can read about them and make up their own minds.

Balanced arguments are easy to structure!

Hey presto! Writing a balanced argument is easy because the structure is very simple. Mugly and Bugly had a quarrel this morning. Here's how I would plan it if I wanted to write it as a balanced argument.

Paragraph 1   The introduction explains what the argument is about, and why it matters.

Mugly wants flies for tea, and Bugly wants snails. Pointy needs to start cooking!

Paragraph 2   First argument in favour of flies

Flies are cheaper, so they can afford huge portions.

Paragraph 3   Second argument in favour of flies

Flies are big and juicy at this time of year.

Paragraph 4   First argument in favour of snails

It's Bugly's turn to choose tea today.

Paragraph 5   Second argument in favour of snails

Snails cost more because they taste better.

Paragraph 6   The conclusion sums up the debate and may suggest a third way to look at the problem.

Whatever Mugly and Bugly have for tea, they'll eat too much and burp all evening. Pointy gave up waiting, and cooked worms.

Don't forget to make sure you have the same number of arguments for and against, and don't favour either point of view in your introduction or conclusion.

Connectives link your arguments together.

We're going to look at how we can use connectives to help our balanced argument make better sense. You can use them to connect two views for or against the topic, or to contrast differing views.

Connectives to add to a point of view

in addition to also

as a result furthermore

Connectives to contrast differing viewpoints

however nevertheless

on the other hand in contrast

Hey presto! Let's see how they work.

Flies are very cheap at this time of year, **in addition to** being fat and juicy.

On the other hand, snails are delicious and, **furthermore**, it's Bugly's turn to choose tea.

 MAGIC WORDS balanced argument

Wizard's Practice

Workbook page 31

Here are three arguments in favour of children having pocket money. Write down two arguments against.

Children enjoy spending their own money.
They can save for things they want.
They will learn the value of money.

1 _____

2 _____

Instructions

There are lots of different types of instructions, including how to build things from a kit, recipes, and directions to help you find a new place. Super!

Order is all-important!

Writing instructions is easy when you know how! Just break the task down into small chunks, and make sure you describe each one in the right order. If you get them round the wrong way, or miss one out, your readers will get in an awful muddle!

Most of the time, the sequence of the steps is really important, so numbering them helps to ensure that your readers do them in the right order.

Always give your instructions a heading, so people know what the instructions are for. You could think about including diagrams or a picture too.

Have a look at these instructions from Wizard Whimstaff's spell book. Can you see how all the steps are numbered? If you got them the wrong way round, you'd turn into a walrus! Super!

To prevent hiccups

1 Mix four weasel whiskers with the tears of an owl.

2 Add the root of poison ivy.

3 Boil slowly in a silver cauldron.

4 Strain the mixture and allow to cool.

5 Swallow a tablespoon at full moon.

 If the order is less important, you may be able to use bullet points instead of numbers. They're good for things like directions too.

You need to say exactly what you mean!

You'll soon get the hang of writing super instructions!

Instructions usually contain **imperative verbs**. These are verbs that give orders, like **strain** the mixture, or **add** the root. They'd probably seem a bit rude in other types of writing, but in instructions they tell the reader exactly what they need to do.

Instructions often contain technical information, like the names of tools or the weights of ingredients. Directions also often contain the names of roads and local landmarks. Make sure you get this information right, because your readers are relying on you!

You might also want to use connectives like **next**, **then**, **afterwards** and **finally**, to link the separate steps together.

MAGIC WORDS | imperative verb

Wizard's Practice

Workbook page 32

Number these instructions for cleaning up at the end of the day.

1. ☐ Finally, close and lock the cupboard door.
2. ☐ Once it is empty, wash the cauldron.
3. ☐ When all the bottles have their lids on, put them in the cupboard.
4. ☐ Firstly, tip any unused potions out of the cauldron.
5. ☐ Put the lids on all the bottles.

Journalistic writing

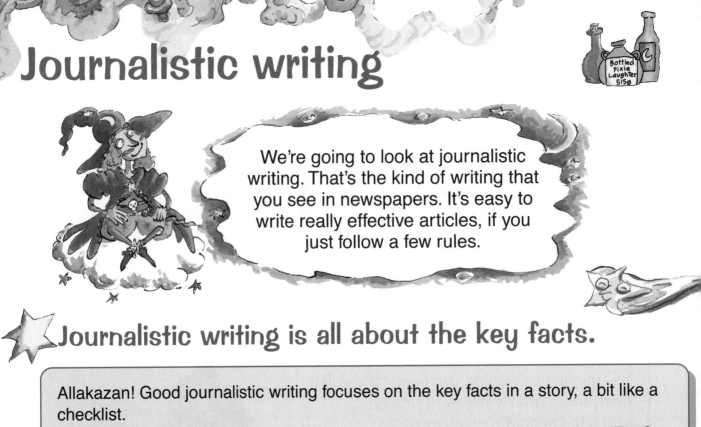

We're going to look at journalistic writing. That's the kind of writing that you see in newspapers. It's easy to write really effective articles, if you just follow a few rules.

Journalistic writing is all about the key facts.

Allakazan! Good journalistic writing focuses on the key facts in a story, a bit like a checklist.

> what?   when?
>
>   who?
>
>   where?
>
> why?   how?

Hey presto! The order you put the information in will depend on the story. Good journalists always put the most important information first, so if a famous person does something, you'd put who did it first, or if something happened at a well-known place, you might talk about the location first.

Of course, you need a headline too. It should sum up what the story is about, but be short and catchy, because it's the first thing the reader sees.

Good headlines tend to be dramatic and often use alliteration or metaphor for extra impact.

Burglars Behind Bars

 Real newspaper stories are always written with the most important information at the top, to draw the readers in.

Stating the facts needn't be boring!

Let me show you how the language you use can make your story more interesting to read.

Journalistic writing should be **objective**. It should present the facts without taking sides. That doesn't mean it has to be boring, though!

Lots of newspaper articles contain creative techniques like alliteration, metaphor and simile too.

Bungling burglar Bill Brown was behind bars this evening after the judge described him as a bad apple. The crook was caught after scaling the side of a house and climbing through an open window, only to find himself at a local police convention.

Arresting officer PC Beat explains: "He climbs like a monkey, but his planning let him down."

alliteration

metaphor

simile

Including a quote from someone involved in the story makes an article more interesting to read and more believable.

MAGIC WORDS | objective

Wizard's Practice

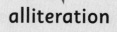
Workbook page 33

Think of creative ways to describe these people in a newspaper report. Try using simile, metaphor and alliteration.

1. A policeman who has won an award. _____

2. A missing pet lamb. _____

3. A man who has broken the world record for sleeping the longest. _____

4. A girl called Tara who has won a talent contest. _____

5. An old age pensioner who has done a parachute jump. _____

Adverts

There are lots of different types of adverts in newspapers and magazines, on TV, the radio and the Internet, and on things like leaflets and billboards. Most adverts don't contain very many words, so you need to make sure that every single one is working really hard!

Adverts aim to persuade the reader.

Writing persuasive adverts is easy when you know how!

Adverts want the product they're advertising to seem really exciting – even if it's toothpaste or toilet cleaner! They also want people to think that it's good value for money.

To do this, adverts encourage readers to imagine how good it would feel to use the product. They often contain lots of superlative adjectives, like **best**, **brightest** or **latest**, and words like **new**, **improved** and **unique**, to make sure their product stands out from their competitors. Super!

New! Soot-be-gone Cauldron Cleaner

Embarrassed by your cauldron? Wish you could see your reflection in it, like other wizards can?

Soot-be-gone's unique formula is the latest thing in cauldron cleansing. The most powerful cleaner on the market, Soot-be-gone will power through the grime to leave an unbelievable shine.

Doesn't your cauldron deserve the best?

Advertisers can promote their products, but they have to tell the truth, and must be able to provide proof for any claims they make.

Adverts inform too!

Adverts need to contain information about the product too, like where you can buy it, or how much it costs.

Don't include more information than you need, but make sure that your reader has all the facts they'd need if they wanted to buy the product or use the service you're advertising. You'll soon get the hang of it!

Eight out of ten frogs prefer Croak Worms!

Available in branches of Spellman Stores and Magic Mart now!

Special introductory price: 80p!

New recipe!

This advert only needs to tell the reader where they can buy the product and how much it costs.

Leaflets for restaurants or attractions might also need to include an address and phone number, opening hours, and a map or directions too.

 Adverts usually contain pictures. In a test you'll only get marks for your writing, though, so don't spend time drawing pictures.

Wizard's Practice

Workbook page 34

Underline the superlative adjectives in these adverts.

1. The fastest broomstick commercially available.
2. Your best magic hat yet or your money back!
3. The very latest development in potion storage.
4. The most reliable frog weight loss programme on the market.
5. The clearest crystal ball you have ever seen.

Recounts

Slurp! **Recounts**, or chronological accounts, record what happened, so that people who weren't there can understand what went on.

Recounts stick to the facts.

Recounts are quite simple to write. They're information texts, so they shouldn't contain your views or opinions – just the facts.

You need to take care to include all of the relevant information, and make sure you record the events in the order in which they happened. You might need to include specific information, such as date and time, or location, so make sure you get these right.

Don't include irrelevant information, because it will just bore or confuse your reader.

Croak! Planning your recount will be easier if you use a paragraph to describe each separate event. Look at Mugly's recount below.

> *I was eating my snails at 9am when Bugly pushed past me, knocking me face-first into my breakfast.*
>
> *I hopped after him because I was cross, but slipped on a snail and skidded into the potions cabinet.*
>
> *Several bottles broke and potion spilt on the floor.*

Recounts should be objective, but reports of the same event written by different people will be quite different, because people have different perspectives. What do you think Bugly's recount would be like?

The language you use is important!

Brain cell alert! The language you use in a recount is important. The language tends to be quite formal, so don't use creative techniques like simile, metaphor or alliteration.

Because recounts are about events that have already happened, you have to use past tense verbs. Choose verbs and adverbs that describe accurately what people did, and use adjectives to describe what they looked like.

> The tall man grabbed the bag and ran quickly
> down the road, towards the park.

Connectives like **first**, **next** and **eventually** can help you to link the events together in a clear order.

> **Afterwards**, the short, plump man followed.
> **Finally**, their snarling dog turned and trotted
> after them.

Remember not to keep using the connective **then**!

MAGIC WORDS   recount

Wizard's Practice

Workbook page 35

Put a tick next to the sentences you would not expect to see in a recount.

1. The train left at 9.15pm. ☐
2. Sammy swims like a fish. ☐
3. Next, the teacher handed out the maths books. ☐
4. The man is the black sheep of the family. ☐
5. I noticed that the little girl had dropped her teddy. ☐

Non-chronological reports

Let me tell you about **non-chronological reports**. They're just reports about a particular topic.

Non-chronological reports are information texts.

Hey presto! Non-chronological reports are information texts, so they describe how things are, rather than trying to persuade the reader to take a particular view.

They're easy to plan. You start with an introduction, which tells the reader what the report is about, and what angle you're taking.

Next, you split your material into topics, with a paragraph for each one. Unlike a recount, it usually doesn't matter what order they go in.

At the end, your conclusion sums up the points you've made.

> Being a Wizard
>
> **Plan**
>
> **Introduction**
> This report is about what it's like to be a wizard.
> Being a wizard can be hard work, but it's lots of fun!
>
> **Paragraph one**
> Training to be a wizard
> • Going to wizard school
> • Conjuring exams
> • Easy spells for beginners
>
> **Paragraph two**
> Choosing equipment
> • Cauldron
> • Wand
> • Hat
>
> **Conclusion**
> You have to work hard to become a wizard and you need to buy lots of equipment, but it's also lots of fun.

☆ You need to use the impersonal voice.

Allakazan! Now let's look at the kind of language you need to use in a non-chronological report.

Non-chronological reports are written in the present tense, using the impersonal voice. That just means you'd write **wizards find a large cauldron useful**, rather than **I find a large cauldron useful**.

Generalisations are useful too, so I might write **many wizards have a spare wand**, or **most hats only last for a few years**.

There will also be specific technical words in the report too, like **cauldron** or **wand**.

You need to use adjectives to describe things, but avoid creative techniques like simile, metaphor or personification. They don't really belong in an information text.

 If you use technical words that might be new to your reader, make sure that you explain what they mean.

MAGIC WORDS non-chronological report · impersonal voice

Wizard's Practice

Workbook page 36

Write **True** or **False** next to these statements about non-chronological reports.

1. Non-chronological reports are written in the past tense. _____

2. You should use the impersonal voice to write them. _____

3. You should use plenty of alliteration. _____

4. You should break your writing into topics, and write a paragraph for each topic. _____

5. You may need to use technical words in your report. _____

Letters

Letters can be formal or informal, depending on who you're writing to. The kind of letter you're writing will affect the layout and the language you use.

⭐ Formal letters need formal language!

Writing formal letters is easy when you know how!

Foundation for Sorcery
Magic Mount
Sylvania
SY12 0TP

18th December 2007

Wizard Whimstaff
"The Cave"
Spellbourne
SP9 4TL

Dear Mr. Whimstaff,

We are writing to ask if you would be kind enough to deliver the keynote speech at the Wizards' Convention to be held next month.

The theme for the convention is 'Unicorn – myth or reality?' It is understood that you are an expert on the subject, and we would be very interested to hear your views.

Your early response would be greatly appreciated.

Yours sincerely,

Wizard Wizen

The address of the person writing a formal letter goes here, with the date below.

The address of the person you're writing to goes here.

If you don't know the person's name, use **Sir** for a man and **Madam** for a woman.

Start by saying why you're writing.

End by saying what you want to happen next.

Finish the letter **Yours sincerely** if you know the name of the person you're writing to. Otherwise finish it **Yours faithfully**.

Formal language checklist: use full names, use passive verbs, don't use contractions, don't use slang.

Informal letters are less complicated!

You'll soon get the hang of writing informal letters, because there are fewer rules to follow! You need to start with your address and the date, like in a formal letter, but you don't need the address of the person you're writing to.

When you start the letter, you can just use the person's first name, and after that what you write is up to you. Super!

You might like to start by asking how the person is, and it's sensible to start a new paragraph each time you start writing about a new topic.

You can finish your letter however you like, too. **Lots of love**, **Take care** and **See you soon** are all good choices. Then you just sign your name. It's easy when you know how!

 Informal language checklist: use first names or Mum/Dad, contractions are fine, use active verbs, some slang is fine (if your reader will understand it!).

Wizard's Practice

Workbook page 37

Practice makes perfect! Would you write a formal or informal letter to these people? Write **Formal** or **Informal** after each one.

1. Your teacher   _____
2. Your best friend   _____
3. Your sister   _____
4. The manager of a local shop   _____
5. A pen pal   _____

Wizard's Challenge

 1 Special effects

> Slurp! Pick a suitable word to complete this passage of alliteration.
>
> Five fish followed _____

 2 More special effects

> Burp! Write a sentence describing a cave setting, using personification.
>
> _____
>
> _____
>
> _____

3 Settings

> Now give one technique you could use to move from one setting to another when you're writing a story.
>
> _____
>
> _____
>
> _____
>
> _____

4 Balanced arguments

Burp! Here's an argument in favour of a new cinema being built in your town. Bet you can't write an argument against it!

> The old cinema only has two screens, so it can't show many films.

_____

_____

_____

_____

5 Adverts

Is it time for a nap yet? Underline the superlative adjectives in this advert, while we have a snooze.

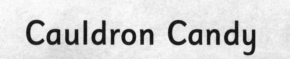

Cauldron Candy

• Best ever recipe!

• Try the latest taste sensation!

Reading skills

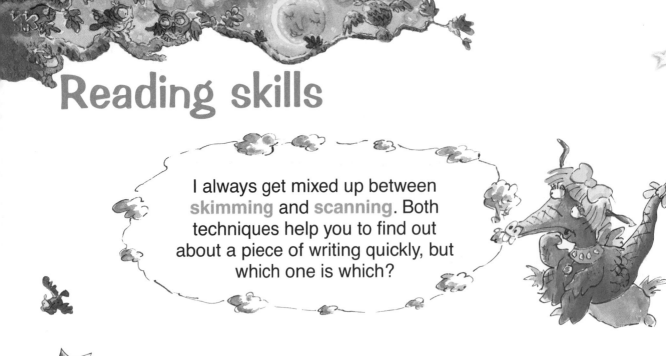

I always get mixed up between **skimming** and **scanning**. Both techniques help you to find out about a piece of writing quickly, but which one is which?

Skimming is just getting to know the text!

I remember! Skimming is where you read through a piece of text really quickly to find out what it's about.

In a test, skimming gives you a good idea of how the information is organised, to help you find specific facts to answer the questions later.

Even if you think you've found the answer to a test question when you're skimming, you should still keep reading through to the end of the piece, in case there's a better answer later on. Then you need to go back to that part of the text and read it again, very carefully, to make sure you understand what it says.

Don't forget to read the questions really carefully in a test. It's easy to pick up marks for locating information, but it's easy to make silly mistakes too!

Scanning is looking for key facts!

Scanning is where you whizz through a piece of text, looking for a specific piece of information you need. For example, a test question might ask what year something happened, so you could look for dates.

Abracadada! If you've done a good job of skimming, you may already know which section of text to look in for the specific piece of information you need. You have to be careful, though, because there may be more than one date in the text, so you need to pick the right one!

MAGIC WORDS **skimming · scanning**

Wizard's Practice

Workbook page 38

Skim and scan through this passage to see how quickly you can find the answers to these questions.

We bought our first rabbits when I was six years old. At first we had a pair of Giant Lops which we took to shows along the south coast. Over the years we've added more rabbits to our collection. My favourite rabbit is little Sooty, who won gold in Belgium a few years back, but the champion is Monty, who has won 15 medals so far.

1. What is the text about?_____

2. How old was the writer when they first had rabbits? _____

3. Where did they start showing their rabbits?_____

4. Which rabbit is the champion?_____

5. Where did Sooty win gold?_____

More reading skills

Good writers leave clues in their writing which help us to understand what's happening and how the characters are feeling. The reading skills we need to find those clues are called **inference and deduction**. Super!

Inference and deduction is just detective work!

Using inference and deduction to understand writing is easy when you know how!

Look at this piece of text.

> Jade gazed out of the window towards the neighbours' garden. She could hear the shouts of children playing, and see the water in their pool glinting in the sunlight, calling to her.
>
> Reluctantly, she dragged herself away from the window and slouched sulkily back to her desk, forcing herself to focus on the waiting books, and driving thoughts of the cool water from her mind.

Reading test papers often ask you why you think a writer chooses specific words.

First, work out what is special about those words. Are they a simile or metaphor? Or perhaps alliteration or personification? Next, think about why you would use that technique in your own writing, to help you answer the question.

For example, you might be asked why you think the writer uses the words **waiting books**. This is personification, because books can't really wait. It creates the idea that, in the end, Jade has to go back to the books, because they're waiting for her!

 Inference and deduction are great for tackling questions on a reading paper where the answer doesn't seem to be in the text.

Use empathy to help you!

To answer other questions, you'll need to understand how a character is feeling. This is called **empathy**. You'll soon get the hang of it!

Very often the writer will have left clues for you, like using the verbs **dragged** and **slouched** in the piece of writing we have just been looking at. Happy people don't usually slouch or drag themselves about, so that gives us a clue about how she's feeling!

We can understand more by thinking how we would feel in Jade's position.

Imagine it was a hot day and you knew that the children next door were playing in their pool. How would you feel if you had to stay inside and work?

So by combining empathy with the clues in the text, we can get to the bottom of how characters are feeling. Super!

Remember, you must use examples from the text to back up your answer. It isn't enough to say that Jade is fed up because you would be if you were in her shoes!

MAGIC WORDS inference and deduction · empathy

Wizard's Practice

Workbook page 39

Write down five verbs the writer uses in the passage to help build up a picture of what is happening.

1. _____
2. _____
3. _____
4. _____
5. _____

Reading fiction

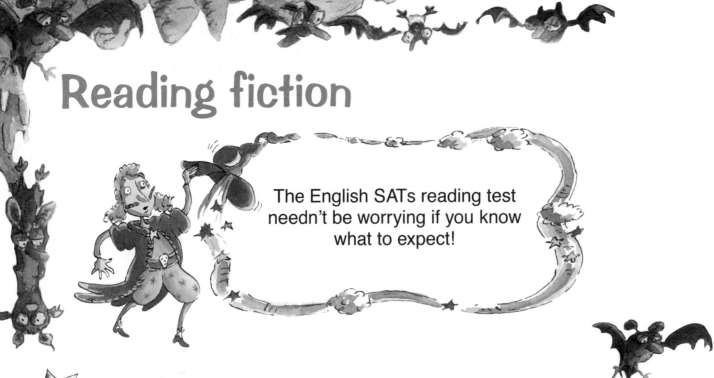

The English SATs reading test needn't be worrying if you know what to expect!

Reading fiction needs special skills!

The reading booklet contains a mixture of fiction, poems and non-fiction writing, all based on a theme. Reading the fiction part of the booklet needs special reading skills.

Fiction writing often uses lots of creative techniques like simile, metaphor, alliteration and personification, and some questions may ask why you think the writer has used them.

You may need to find clues in the text that tell you what characters are like or how they're feeling.

All of this means that you'll probably need to use inference and deduction to uncover some of the answers.

As you read, makes notes in the margin about the things you notice, and underline the characters' names, important events, and changes in location.

Try to answer the questions in order, as each one builds on the understanding you used to answer the previous one.

Looking at the pictures will help you to remember what happened on each page.

You'll need to answer different types of questions.

Now let me tell you about the different types of questions you might have to answer.

Multiple-choice questions are usually worth one mark. Just pick the best answer from a selection!

Hey presto! Other one-mark questions just need one word or a short sentence answer. You might have to find a piece of information, or say why a character feels a certain way.

Two-mark questions tend to need three or four sentences. You might have to give a couple of reasons why the writer chose a particular phrase and how it builds up a picture.

With three-mark questions, you have to give a full explanation, with evidence from the text to back it up. If you needed to say how you know that a character is homesick, you'd have to find examples of words or phrases that tell you, and say how they create the idea.

Do your best with three-mark questions. Even if you don't get all three marks, you could still get one or two valuable marks.

Wizard's Practice

Workbook page 40

Write **True** or **False** next to these statements.

1. With multiple-choice questions, you have to pick the two best answers. _____

2. Two-mark questions often need answers that are three or four sentences long. _____

3. Fiction writing includes lots of creative techniques. _____

4. Three-mark questions need examples from the text to back up your ideas. _____

5. There are no characters in fiction writing. _____

Reading non-fiction

Burp! The SATs reading paper will contain non-fiction texts too. So be prepared! Slurp!

Reading non-fiction needs different skills.

Brain cell alert! Reading non-fiction needs a different set of skills.

To start with, there are lots of different types of non-fiction text, so you need to decide which one you're reading. The title will probably give you some clues. **Assembling your new bike** is likely to be instructions; **Roman Roads** will probably be a non-chronological report.

Croak! The structure of the text is important too. Is it all in paragraphs, or are there some bullet points, or sections of boxed text? Are there sub-headings, tables, or diagrams? Why has the writer chosen to organise the information this way and how does it help the reader? Look out for changes in the type of text.

Other questions might ask why the writer has chosen a particular word or phrase.

For example, you might be asked why the writer of a new soap powder advert used the phrase '**For whites you can be proud of**'. You'd need to use inference and deduction to spot that if people are proud of really white clothes, they might be ashamed if their whites come out a bit grey! The new soap powder promises to spare them that embarrassment. Burp!

There are four main types of questions on the paper.

Yawn! We're off for a nap now, while you have a look at the different kinds of questions you'll need to answer!

Multiple-choice questions are worth one mark. You have to pick the best answer from a selection.

Other one-mark questions may ask you to find a specific piece of information, say what kind of text it is, or why the title was chosen. One word, or a short sentence, is enough.

Two-mark questions might ask you to find related pieces of information or explain why something happened the way it did.

Three-mark questions need a longer answer, backed up with evidence from the text. You might be asked to find two different techniques the writer has used to organise the text, then comment on why they chose each one, and how they help the reader.

The answer booklet will tell you where to look in the reading booklet to find the information you need for each question.

Wizard's Practice

Workbook page 41

Write down five different features a non-fiction writer might use to organise the text.

1 _____

2 _____

3 _____

4 _____

5 _____

Reading poetry

You can be prepared for any poetry that may be on the SATs reading paper, by brushing up your poetry reading skills. Practice makes perfect.

⭐ Poems are crammed with meaning!

Understanding poetry is easy when you know how! Poems contain far fewer words than a story, so poets choose their language really carefully to pack as much meaning as they can into a few words.

Because of that, reading test papers ask lots of questions about how the words in the poem help to create atmosphere.

Read the poem through quickly to begin with, to give you an idea of what it's about. The title may give you a clue as well.

After that, go back and read the whole poem again carefully. Draw boxes round the different verses or sections, and give each one a label which sums up what it's about. Perhaps the atmosphere has changed or a new idea is being explored.

Next, think about the creative techniques that the poet has used. Underline examples of alliteration and personification, and any other special effects you notice. Think about how they add to the atmosphere the poet is trying to create.

Just like fiction, the answers to questions about poetry won't always be obvious straight away. You'll probably need to use inference and deduction to find the information you need.

Try writing your own poems. It'll help you to understand how language is used to create atmosphere in poetry.

The reading paper contains questions on poetry too!

Reading test papers have the same four types of questions for poetry as they do for fiction and non-fiction texts. Super!

Multiple-choice questions, worth one mark, might ask you to pick the best phrase to describe how a poem describes its subject, from a selection of options.

Short questions, worth one mark, might ask why the poet has chosen to use a particular technique.

Two-mark questions might ask you to find two examples of where a poet has created a particular effect.

Long three-mark questions might ask you to explain how the atmosphere of the poem differs between two verses. You would need to describe the atmosphere in each verse and say how they differ, with examples from the poem to support your view. You might also say how the change affects how the poem as a whole works.

Wizard's Practice

Workbook page 42

Circle the features that you might find in a poem.

1. verses
2. alliteration
3. bullet points
4. personification
5. sub-headings

Wizard's Challenge

1 Reading skills

Burp! Use your reading skills to answer the questions about this piece of text.

When fire broke out in Pudding Lane on September 2nd 1666, Lord Mayor Thomas Bludworth dismissed it as insignificant. His mistake would bring London to its knees. The fire quickly spread beyond all control and by the time the final blaze was put out, on September 6th, the Great Fire had claimed four fifths of the city, destroying 13,200 houses.

a What is the text about? _____

b What date did the fire first break out? _____

c Who mistakenly thought it would be a small fire? _____

d What does the writer mean by the word **claimed** in the fourth line?

_____

2 Reading fiction

Slurp! Read this piece of fiction writing, then answer the questions.

My heart sank as the car slowed to a halt, joining a queue that stretched into the hazy distance like a reptile, belching fumes. Hadn't I said this would happen?

I pictured my friends. They'd be tucking into pizza right now!

a What is happening in this text? _____

b Why does the writer say the traffic queue is like a reptile? _____

c What is the effect of the word **belching**? _____

d How do you know the narrator did not want to take this trip? _____

3 Reading non-fiction

Grub's up! Answer the questions, while we grab a snack!

> ## Perfection in Paris!
>
> The newly opened Metro Hotel represents the very best of French hospitality. This luxuriously appointed hotel is centrally located, offering business travellers and tourists alike unparalleled access to landmarks like the Eiffel Tower and Arc de Triomphe.
>
> **Facilities**
> - Indoor swimming pool
> - 5-star restaurant
> - Home cinema system in suites

a What is the purpose of this text? _____

b Why did the writer choose the title **Perfection in Paris**? _____

_____

c Find two adverbs which help to promote the hotel. _____ _____

d Why has the writer used bullet points to present the information about the facilities? _____

4 Reading poetry

Join these lines from poems with the creative technique they contain.

a Mist melting momentarily, then rolling in again   simile

b The plish plash of rain on the roof   metaphor

c Sleek like a cat, she slips away   onomatopoeia

d Wet leaves wink in spring sunshine   alliteration

e Whirling on satin-tipped toes, she is a star   personification

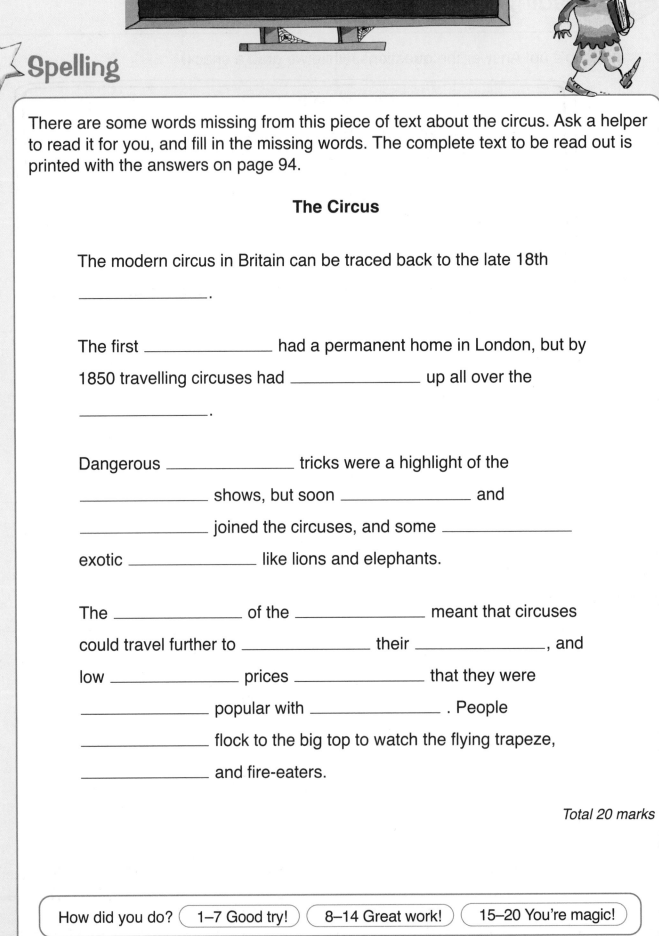

⭐ Spelling

There are some words missing from this piece of text about the circus. Ask a helper to read it for you, and fill in the missing words. The complete text to be read out is printed with the answers on page 94.

The Circus

The modern circus in Britain can be traced back to the late 18th

_____.

The first _____ had a permanent home in London, but by

1850 travelling circuses had _____ up all over the

_____.

Dangerous _____ tricks were a highlight of the

_____ shows, but soon _____ and

_____ joined the circuses, and some _____

exotic _____ like lions and elephants.

The _____ of the _____ meant that circuses

could travel further to _____ their _____, and

low _____ prices _____ that they were

_____ popular with _____ . People

_____ flock to the big top to watch the flying trapeze,

_____ and fire-eaters.

Total 20 marks

How did you do? (1–7 Good try!) (8–14 Great work!) (15–20 You're magic!)

 **Writing**

Read this story opening, then answer the questions.

Adventure on the Underground

The tube train slowed down as it approached the platform and the doors slid open. Good, lots of free seats! I hopped onto the train and turned round to see Mum still gathering up shopping bags on the platform.

The doors closed, and Mum was left behind. Even worse, she had my ticket, and the ticket inspector was coming!

Write down some direct speech that might happen between the narrator and the ticket inspector.

Narrator

_____

(1 mark for appropriate language, 1 mark for correct speech punctuation)

Ticket Inspector

_____

(1 mark for appropriate language, 1 mark for correct speech punctuation)

Narrator

_____

(1 mark for appropriate language, 1 mark for correct speech punctuation)

Apart from the ticket inspector, can you think of two other problems that the narrator might face?

_____

(1 mark)

_____

(1 mark)

Write down two phrases you could use to describe the underground station.

_____

(1 mark)

_____

(1 mark)

How did you do? (1–4 Good try!) (5–8 Great work!) (9–10 You're magic!)

Reading

River Revival

A group of 'green' local residents have transformed a stretch of river, with amazing results. The section of the River Bourne which flows behind the town centre had become so overgrown that rubbish had collected, encouraging rats into the area.

Now the stream has swapped rats for rare water voles, thanks to the efforts of Frank Simms and his neighbours, whose gardens back onto the stream.

"This part of the stream is difficult to get to, but when we saw the rats, we knew we had to take action. We cleared out all the weeds and rubbish, and it's so pretty now that some of us are taking down our back fences, so we can enjoy the view!"

Following the clean-up, the council has pledged to clear further stretches of river.

Choose the best phrase to complete this sentence.

1 The stream had become overgrown because...

- it ran behind the town centre
- it was difficult to get to
- it ran at the end of Frank Simms' garden
- rats had been attracted to it

(1 mark)

2 Why are the neighbours described as 'green' local residents?

_____

(1 mark)

3 What made Frank and his neighbours decide to take action?

_____

(1 mark)

4 Why has the writer included a quote from Frank Simms?

_____

(1 mark)

5 Give three reasons why you think the writer chose the headline **River Revival**.

_____

_____

(3 marks)

6 List three 'amazing results' of the river clean-up.

_____

_____

(3 marks)

Beautiful Beach

As Alex walked Zach along the beach, he looked at the rubbish. A plastic bottle trundled along in the breeze and an old newspaper waved forlornly by a breakwater. Crinkling carriers crashed in and out with the waves and a broken jar lay in wait for the next pair of soft, bare feet.

Alex thought, if people were at home, instead of at the beach, all of this rubbish would go to the recycling centre.

And then inspiration: "I know what this beach needs, Zach!"

1 Who or what is Zach?

_____

(1 mark)

2 Why do you think the writer says that the old newspaper waved **forlornly**?

_____

(1 mark)

3 Give two reasons why the writer used the verb **crinkling** to describe the carrier bags.

_____

_____

(2 marks)

4 What was Alex's idea?

_____

(1 mark)

5 Give an example of evidence in the text to support your idea.

_____

_____

(1 mark)

How did you do? (1–6 Good try!) (7–12 Great work!) (13–16 You're magic!)

Answers

Page 5

1 Miss Snufflebeam can't breathe fire yet.
2 Mugly and Bugly doze because they're lazy.
3 Wizard Whimstaff's magic is amazing.
4 It's dark in the cave.
5 Six rats' tails went into the spell.

Page 7

1 dang<u>e</u>rous
2 off<u>e</u>ring
3 bound<u>a</u>ry
4 diff<u>e</u>rence
5 gen<u>e</u>ral

Page 9

1 married
2 relying
3 steadily
4 silliness
5 dries

Page 11

1 hid
2 fought
3 brought
4 spoke
5 knew

Page 13

Sentences that should be ticked are:
2 Miss Snufflebeam said, "Oh dear! I've made a mistake."
3 "This is hard work!" complained Mugly and Bugly.
5 "Bugly, have you eaten all of the flies?" demanded Mugly.

Page 15

Correct homophones are:
1 ate
2 reads
3 ball
4 for
5 poured

Page 17

Many answers are possible. An adult helper should check the child's understanding of different noun types.

Page 19

1 The cat appeared at the door, so <u>she</u> let <u>it</u> in.
2 Mugly and Bugly fell asleep after <u>they</u> had eaten.

3 Pointy can't remember where <u>he</u> put the cauldron.
4 Miss Snufflebeam was bored, so Pointy played a game with <u>her</u>.
5 Mugly and Bugly made a mess, so Pointy cleared up after <u>them</u>.

Page 21

1 True
2 False
3 True
4 False
5 True

Page 23

1 Mugly is fat, <u>but</u> Bugly is fatter.
2 Miss Snufflebeam was confused <u>because</u> the work was hard.
3 Wizard Whimstaff grabbed his wand <u>before</u> he cast the spell.
4 Pointy made Mugly and Bugly a snack <u>so</u> they would stop complaining.
5 The bats flew out of the cave <u>although</u> it was still light outside.

Page 25

1 excitedly
2 curiously
3 politely
4 sulkily
5 proudly

Page 27

1 over
2 under
3 after
4 before
5 in

Page 29

1 spells
2 wishes
3 families
4 teeth
5 species

Page 31

1 <u>While Mugly was asleep</u>, Bugly ate all of the food.
2 Wizard Whimstaff, <u>who is a wonderful wizard</u>, cast a powerful spell.
3 <u>Whistling to himself</u>, Pointy stirred the cauldron.
4 Miss Snufflebeam skipped off to play, <u>blowing little puffs of smoke</u>.
5 Mugly and Bugly, <u>croaking loudly</u>, hopped onto a lily pad.

Page 33

1 Blowing puffs of smoke, Miss Snufflebeam skipped out of the cave.
2 "Mugly and Bugly have made a mess again," grumbled Pointy.
3 Wizard Whimstaff, with his wand held high, said the magic words.
4 Mugly and Bugly ate six flies, three snails and a plate of swamp slime.
5 Pointy washed up the potion bottles, singing cheerfully.

Page 35

The words that should be circled are:
1 Snufflebeam
2 It
3 Tuesday
4 Transylvania
5 I

Page 37

1 impolite
2 disapprove
3 indecisive
4 uncertain
5 antiseptic

Pages 38–39

Wizard's Challenge

1 Miss Snufflebeam's smoke got into Pointy's eyes, so he didn't see the crystal ball until he'd knocked it off its stand.

2 a parli<u>a</u>ment
  b diff<u>e</u>rent
  c ref<u>e</u>rence
  d nat<u>u</u>ral

3 a ran
  b joked
  c crept

4 Miss Snufflebeam won't be able to blow smoke until she's older.

5 a whispered → shyly
  b shouted → angrily
  c asked → pleadingly

6 a lady → change y to i and add es
  b box → add es
  c train → add s

Page 41

Answers will vary, but strong ones will describe a credible chain of events to lead Wendy back home safely.

Page 43
1 A
2 O
3 O
4 A
5 A

Page 45
1 picture
2 lamb
3 wind
4 mouse
5 fish

Page 47
Several answers are possible, but may include:
1 ancient
2 giggle
3 stroll
4 brave
5 shatter

Page 49
1 Informal
2 Formal
3 Informal
4 Informal
5 Formal

Page 51
Endings will vary.

Page 53
Answers will vary, but may include:
athletic, quick as a flash, skilful, determined, legendary

Page 55
1 a hospital ward → gleaming tiles
2 a woodland → lush leaves
3 a beach → crunching pebbles
4 a classroom → pointy pencils poised
5 a swimming pool   excited splashing

Page 57
1 She hates her little brother.
2 He drives her mad.
3 He's always stealing her things.
4 He makes the whole house a mess.
5 She does think he's cute when he's asleep, though!

Page 59
1 Fiction: fantasy quest
2 Non-fiction: instructions
3 Non-fiction: advert
4 Non-fiction: journalistic writing
5 Fiction: thriller

Page 61
Answers will vary, but may include:
Children will spend all their money on sweets, which are bad for them.
Children might lose their money or have it stolen.

Page 63
1 5
2 2
3 4
4 1
5 3

Page 65
Answers will vary. Possible answers are:
1 proud policeman
2 lost lamb
3 super sleeper
4 talented Tara
5 parachuting pensioner

Page 67
The <u>fastest</u> broomstick commercially available.
Your <u>best</u> magic hat yet or your money back!
The <u>very latest</u> development in potion storage.
The <u>most reliable</u> frog weight loss programme on the market.
The <u>clearest</u> crystal ball you have ever seen.

Page 69
Sentences that should be ticked are:
2 Sammy swims like a fish.
4 The man is the black sheep of the family.

Page 71
False
True
False
True
True

Page 73
1 Formal
2 Informal
3 Informal
4 Formal
5 Informal

Pages 74–75
Wizard's Challenge
1 Many answers are possible, including:
Five fish followed frantically.
2 Many answers are possible, but may include:
We walked towards the yawning cave, its dark interior waiting to enfold us.
3 Time connectives, e.g. meanwhile, at the same time, later that day.
4 Many answers are possible, but may include:
The old cinema will go out of business and the people who work there will lose their jobs.
5 Cauldron Candy
<u>Best</u> ever recipe!
Try the <u>latest</u> taste sensation!

Page 77
1 showing rabbits
2 six
3 along the south coast
4 Monty
5 in Belgium

Page 79
Answers may be any of these verbs:
gazed
playing
glinting
dragged
slouched
forcing
driving
calling
waiting

Page 81
1 False
2 True
3 True
4 True
5 False

Answers should include five of the following:

bullet points

boxed information

headings

sub-headings

paragraphs

tables

diagrams

Page 85

Features that should be circled are: verses, alliteration, personification.

Pages 86–87

Wizard's Challenge

1 a The Great Fire of London

   b September 2nd 1666

   c Lord Mayor Thomas Bludworth

   d destroyed

2 Good answers may include:

   a The narrator is stuck in a traffic jam.

   b Because the queue of traffic looks like a snake, and snakes are reptiles

   c Belching creates an unpleasant image. It suggests that lots of fumes were escaping, and belching is also a nasty habit.

   d The narrator says she had warned that they would get stuck in traffic, suggesting that she didn't want to take the trip. Also, her friends are having fun without her, and she would prefer to be with them.

3 Good answers may include:

   a to advertise the Metro Hotel

   b Perfection in Paris is alliteration, which attracts the reader. The word perfection also implies that the hotel is perfect.

   c newly, luxuriously

   d Bullet points help to draw attention to each feature.

4 a alliteration

   b onomatopoeia

   c simile

   d personification

   e metaphor

SATs Practice

Page 88

Spelling

The Circus

The modern circus in Britain can be traced back to the late 18th **century**.

The first **circus** had a permanent home in London, but by 1850 travelling circuses had **sprung** up all over the **country**.

Dangerous **riding** tricks were a highlight of the **early** shows, but soon **jugglers** and **acrobats** joined the circuses, and some **imported** exotic **animals** like lions and elephants.

The **arrival** of the **railways** meant that circuses could travel further to **entertain** their **audiences**, and low **ticket** prices **meant** that they were **hugely** popular with **families**. People **would** flock to the big top to watch the flying trapeze, **clowns** and fire-eaters.

Page 89

Writing

Adventure on the Underground

Direct speech should use appropriate language and correct speech punctuation. Plot ideas should follow on from the story opening in a convincing way.

Pages 90–91

Reading

Section 1

These questions are about the newspaper article **River Revival**.

1 The stream had become overgrown because it was difficult to get to.

2 The local residents are referred to as being 'green' because they care about the environment, and 'green' is a term used for people or things that protect the environment.

3 Seeing rats by the river made Frank and his neighbours decide to take action.

4 Quotes make stories more interesting to read.

5 i Good answers may recognise that the headline uses alliteration to attract the reader.

   ii It is also short and catchy.

   iii It sums up what the story is about, because the word revival means bringing back to life, and the local residents bring their stretch of river back to life.

6 Any three from the following:

   The rats have gone.

   Rare water voles live there now.

   It is so pretty now that residents are taking down their fences to enjoy the view.

   The council has pledged to clear more of the river.

Section 2

These questions are about the piece of writing **Beautiful Beach**.

1 Zach is a dog.

2 The author chooses the word forlornly to describe the bag because it means abandoned or alone, and the bag had been left behind as rubbish on the beach.

3 Good answers may recognise that crinkling carriers is alliteration.

   It is also onomatopoeia. Both techniques are designed to draw attention to the carrier bags.

4 A good answer would recognise that Alex's idea is to establish recycling facilities at the beach.

5 The evidence in the text is that he thinks about how all of the rubbish is recyclable, and that if people were at home, it would all go to the recycling centre. He then says that he knows what the beach needs, implying that it needs a recycling centre of its own.

Glossary

abstract noun a concept or idea, e.g. love, bravery

active verb a verb that describes who is doing the action, e.g. Ben put the books away

adjective a word or phrase that describes a noun (see also comparative adjective and superlative adjective)

adverb a word or phrase that describes a verb, e.g. run quickly, very tired

alliteration a phrase where most or all of the words begin with the same sound, e.g. Bonny babies bounce beautifully

antonym a word with a meaning opposite to another, e.g. hot, cold

apostrophe a punctuation mark used for contraction, when two words are joined, or to show possession, e.g. Don't take Mary's bag

balanced argument a piece of non-fiction writing designed to explain opposing points of view, i.e. where the writer does not favour one opinion over another

clause a distinct part of a sentence including a verb (see subordinate clause and embedded clause)

collective noun a noun that names a group of people or things, e.g. crowd of people, troupe of monkeys

comma a punctuation mark that shows when to pause, separates clauses, or separates items in a list

common noun a noun that names ordinary things, e.g. cat, table

comparative adjective an adjective that describes a degree of a quality, e.g. more beautiful, taller

complex sentence a sentence that contains a main clause and a subordinate clause

compound sentence a sentence that contains two equally weighted clauses, joined together with a conjunction

conjunction a word used to link sentences or clauses, or to connect words within a phrase, e.g. because, but, later

connective a word or phrase used to connect different parts of a text

consonant any letter of the alphabet except the vowels, a, e, i, o and u

contraction when words are shortened, or two words are joined, by removing letters and replacing with an apostrophe, e.g. don't, you're

dialogue a spoken or written conversation between two people

direct speech words that are actually spoken, enclosed in speech marks

embedded clause a clause that is placed in the middle of a sentence

empathy the ability to understand how other people are feeling

exclamation mark a punctuation mark that can be used instead of a full stop to indicate surprise or that an order has been made, e.g. Hey! Stop that!

fable a story written to give a moral message

fiction stories with imaginary characters, settings or events

full stop a punctuation mark that signals the end of a sentence

genre a style or type of writing. Text can belong to more than one genre, e.g. historical romance

homophone a word which sounds the same as another word but has a different meaning and spelling, e.g. wear, where

imperative verb a verb that gives an order or instruction, e.g. Take a piece of paper

impersonal voice a writing style which describes what people or groups generally do or think, rather than the thoughts or action of an individual, e.g. Most people own a TV. Used for non-chronological reports

indent to start a new paragraph slightly in from the end of a new line. The first paragraph in a text is not indented

inference and deduction when the reader uses their own knowledge, and the imagery created by the author, to read beyond the explicit meaning of the text

main clause the main part of a sentence. It makes sense on its own

metaphor where a writer describes something as if it were something else, e.g. he is a dark horse

narrator the person from whose viewpoint a story is told. May or may not be a character in the story

non-chronological report a report based on a topic rather than a chain of events

non-fiction writing that is not fictional, including information texts about real people and places, letters, instructions and reports

noun a word that names a thing or feeling

objective an objective argument or viewpoint presents the facts but does not take sides

onomatopoeia when a word sounds like the noise it describes, e.g. plop, rustle, crunch

paragraph a section of a piece of writing. New paragraphs signal a change in topic, place or time, or that a new person is speaking (see also indent)

passive verb a verb which describes the actions, e.g. The books were put away by Ben

past tense describes things which have happened

personal pronoun a word used instead of a noun to reduce repetition, e.g. I, you, they we, us

personification a writing technique in which human characteristics are used to describe non-human things, e.g. The branches of the tree reached out to us

phrase two or more words that act as a unit

plural more than one of something. Usually made by adding s, es or ies, e.g. cars, bushes, babies. There are some exceptions, e.g. people, children

prefix a group of letters added to the beginning of a word to change its meaning, e.g. unhappy, disobedient

preposition shows how one thing relates to another, e.g. on, under, through, from

present tense describes things which are happening now

pronoun a word used instead of a noun to avoid having to use the same noun again, e.g. them, you, my, that

proper noun describes a specific person, thing or place, e.g. Kyle, London, Tuesday

question mark a punctuation mark used in place of a full stop to show that a question has been asked

recount a chronological report

reported speech speech reported in a text, but not directly quoted, e.g. He said he would be late

root word a word that you can add a prefix or suffix to

scanning reading quickly to find a specific piece of information

sentence a unit of text that makes sense on its own (see also simple sentence, compound sentence and complex sentence)

simile where a writer compares something to something else, e.g. as clean as a whistle, sleeping like a baby

simple sentence contains only one clause

singular one of something e.g. a dog, the girl

skimming reading quickly to understand the main meaning of a text

speech marks punctuation marks that surround direct speech. Other punctuation goes inside them, e.g. "Hello!" said Ian

subordinate clause adds extra information but does not make sense on its own, e.g. The cat, which was ginger, leapt onto the wall

suffix a group of letters added to the end of a root word to change its meaning, e.g. helpless, boldly

superlative adjective an adjective that describes the extent of a quality, e.g. the biggest, the most or least expensive

syllable a beat within a word, e.g. ca-rrot

synonym a word with the same or similar meaning as another word, e.g. cold, chilly

tense tells us when something is happening

thesaurus a book of synonyms

verb a doing or being word (see also active verb, imperative verb and passive verb)

vowel a, e, i, o or u. The other letters in the alphabet are consonants